# A SHORT HISTORY

## OF

## AMERICAN LAW ENFORCEMENT

# A SHORT HISTORY

## OF

# AMERICAN LAW ENFORCEMENT

*By*

### WILLIAM J. BOPP, M.A.

*Assistant Professor of Law Enforcement*
*Florida Technological University*
*Orlando, Florida*
*Formerly*
*Dade County (Florida) Public Safety Department*
*Oakland (California) Police Department*

*and*

### DONALD O. SCHULTZ, M.P.A.

*Police Science Instructor*
*Broward Community College*
*Fort Lauderdale, Florida*
*Formerly*
*Orange (California) Police Department*

CHARLES C THOMAS • PUBLISHER

*Springfield • Illinois • U.S.A.*

*Published and Distributed Throughout the World by*

CHARLES C THOMAS ● PUBLISHER

BANNERSTONE HOUSE

301-327 East Lawrence Avenue, Springfield, Illinois, U.S.A.

© *1972 by* CHARLES C THOMAS ● PUBLISHER

ISBN 0-398-02237-2 (cloth)

ISBN 0-398-02479-0 (paper)

Library of Congress Catalog Card Number 71-180805

*With* THOMAS BOOKS *careful attention is given to all details of manufacturing and design. It is the Publisher's desire to present books that are satisfactory as to their physical qualities and artistic possibilities and appropriate for their particular use.* THOMAS BOOKS *will be true to those laws of quality that assure a good name and good will.*

*Printed in the United States of America*

*00-2*

*Dedicated to the far-sighted police administrators of old whose courage and scrupulous honesty laid the foundation for the police profession.*

# PREFACE

The purpose of this book is to fill a void created by the absence of an historical American law enforcement text, a fact that was sadly learned when, in a fit of altruism, the authors tried to beef up an introductory law enforcement course with a liberal dose of police history. A search of all the appropriate bibliographies revealed that there simply was no contemporary volume on the subject. Those books that did cover police history generally did so in a haphazard, disoriented manner, choosing to devote more space to "Peelian Reform" than to the entire history of American policing.

The authors began assembling material for a lesson plan on the subject—perhaps one-hundred volumes were accumulated, along with countless editions of journals and periodicals and a sizeable stack of photocopied newspaper stories, all of which covered one or another phase of law enforcement. Yet, even with this sizeable mass of material, there were still gaps in the overall historical experience. So letters were sent to some 350 police departments, large and small, serving all levels of government in every region of the country. The message: send us your history. Almost all of the agencies responded; and when the returns were in, a wealth of material had been forwarded—mimiographed histories, lesson plans, ancient newspaper clippings, old photographs, legislative enactments, personal letters, monographs, crime commission reports, booklets, illustrations, departmental logs. It was then that the authors decided to write this book.

The authors are not, by any stretch of the imagination, historians, nor do they seek to lay any claim to that title. But American policing is 350 years old, and it is no longer practical to wait for the historian to write on the subject, nor is it reasonable to demand that students of the discipline pore through scores of books and hundreds of departmental histories to obtain an overview of police history. The movement to professionalize the police service is at full throttle, and tens of of thousands of law enforcement students are graduating and seeking careers in a field whose history they little know or understand. The authors feel strongly that one of the keys to professionalization is knowledge, knowledge which offers a perspective on the future by focusing on the past.

Abraham Lincoln once said, "We cannot escape history." He was right! History is life, life in the past, and our conceptions of past truths will have a direct effect on our attitudes toward the future. To determine where one is going it is first necessary to survey where one has been. Law enforcement, in order to reach the heady status of a profession, must become increasingly introspective. It is hoped that in some small way this book will contribute to the goal we all cherish—the police profession.

William J. Bopp
Donald O. Schultz

# ACKNOWLEDGMENTS

**P**articular gratitude is expressed to Payne Thomas who reprinted this work from *Principles of American Law Enforcement and Criminal Justice* in order to allow for its use as a supplementary text. To those 285 police departments who forwarded their histories, we are most indebted. Sincere appreciation is given to the library staff of Florida Technological University who by hook, by crook, and through the interlibrary loan system gathered much of the material, some of it very rare, that made this book possible. Our thanks to Judy Reed, who typed the manuscript.

Space limitations constrain us from listing all the people and agencies that assisted us in our work. This we regret! But two very special contributors must be acknowledged. Only those who have published a book will understand the deep debt of gratitude we owe to Sharon Bopp and Pat Schultz, without whose patience and understanding this book would not have been written.

# CONTENTS

# A SHORT HISTORY

## OF

# AMERICAN LAW ENFORCEMENT

Upper part of the pillar upon which the legendary Code of Hammurabi was inscribed.

*Chapter 1*

# BACKGROUNDS AND BEGINNINGS (TO 1607)

T he history of American law enforcement is fairly short, if dated from the first enduring English settlement in the early seventeenth century. Since then, only some three centuries and threescore years have passed—a period that can be spanned by the overlapping lives of five or six men. But of course the American story actually begins many centuries before the New World was colonized. Accordingly, it will do well to review briefly certain early foreign developments.

### THE EARLY EXPERIENCE

Since ancient times man has tried to develop methods of dealing with individuals who committed acts deemed harmful to their communities. The basic concept of law enforcement can be traced back to the dawn of history, where tribal customs embodied the idea of mutual protection through law and order. In essence, the people were the first police, and no other kind was necessary. Intertribal crime was often handled through retaliatory measures (branding, torture, disfigurement) initiated by the aggrieved party—assuming he had survived—or his family. This early type of enforcement led to the idea of *kin police,* whereby the responsibility for obtaining justice rested with a victim's family.[1]

Mesopotamia (Iraq), in a far-reaching innovation, promulgated a succession of legal codes, of which the most famous was the *Code of Hammurabi,* named after the King of Babylon (1947 B.C.–1905 B.C.). The code, engraved on a pillar of stone, specified laws governing the conduct of the King's subjects. It contained provisions on crimes of sex and personal violence, a law against sorcery, and a scale of penalties for violations of each

---

[1]A. C. Germann, Frank D. Day, and Robert R. J. Gallati, *Introduction To Law Enforcement and Criminal Justice* (Springfield: Charles C Thomas, Publisher, 1970), p. 39.

provision. The *Code of Hammurabi* was comprised of some 4,000 lines of writing which were preceded by a poetic prologue of one long sentence that ended with the lofty phrase: "Law and justice I establish in the land and promote the welfare of the people." The code shows a certain systematic order. Beginning with accusation of murder and sorcery, it passes through all grades of social and domestic life, ending with a scale of wages for all classes of workmen, even the lowliest. The three essential features of the code may be clearly defined. First, it was based on individual responsibility under the law. Hence, if a free man destroyed the eye of another, his eye would be destroyed. The second essential feature of the code was the belief in the sanctity of the oath before God, and the third was the absolute necessity of written evidence in all legal matters.

The early Greek city states saw some developments in the dual areas of law and enforcement. In 593 B.C. Solon was elected chief magistrate of Athens, whereupon he initiated a series of fundamental reforms, including the prohibition of slavery for indebtedness, the division of the population into classes based on property, and the granting of full citizenship to even the lowest classes. By this time the law of the land was being *written.* The administration of justice was the responsibility of the Heliaea, juries chosen by lot from among 6,000 representatives of the Athenian tribes. Aggrieved parties took their claims to the Heliasts, who voted in secret ballot for conviction or acquittal. The law specified that in no case would a trial last more than one day.[2]

The most significant innovations, however, were made by the Romans. The development of law is perhaps the greatest of Roman achievements and one that probably best survived into modern times. According to tradition, the legal affairs of ancient Rome were in the hands of patrician magistrates who had succeeded the kings. In the fifth Century B.C. the people demanded the publication of the laws and the abolition of patrician privileges. In response to public pressure, a committee of ten distinguished citizens compiled a code based on Roman customs, and in 451 B.C. it was set up on ten bronze or wooden tablets in the

---

[2]Wallace K. Ferguson and Geofrey Bruun, *Ancient Times To 1520,* 4th ed. (Boston: Houghton Mifflin Company, 1969), pp. 28-29.

Forum. Two more tablets were added a year later. These twelve tablets formed the basis of Roman civil law. The opening passage of the code placed the responsibility for enforcement of the law in the hands of individual citizens and in the courts:[3]

> If a man is summoned to court and does not go, let witnesses be called and then let the plaintiff seize him. If he resists or runs away, let the plaintiff lay hands on him. If he is ill or aged, let the plaintiff provide an animal to carry him.

During the time of the Roman Empire the sources of law developed and changed in various ways. The most important enactments were *leges* (legislation), which were rules laid down by the emperor, or pronouncements of the assembly. Decrees passed by a majority vote of the Senate were called *senatus consulta.* It was also customary for consuls, magistrates, and governors to issue edicts on taking office, giving their interpretation of the law and the action they would take or permit in various circumstances. In 27 B.C. a military police unit, The Praetorian Guard, was created to maintain security at the emperor's palace. The emperor later created the first nonmilitary police force by forming the Vigiles of Rome, a group of a thousand or so men whose job it was to keep peace in the city and to fight fires. The edicts of individual Roman magistrates were exhibited in the Forum and, although each one only affected the issuing magistrate, it became usual for other magistrates to adopt most of a predecessor's edicts. In 130 A.D. the emperor instructed jurists to codify this praetorian law into permanent law under the title *Edictum Perpetuum.*[4]

## ANGLO-SAXON CONTRIBUTIONS

In 500 A.D., when the Germanic tribes (Anglo-Saxons) from central Europe invaded England, they brought with them a tribal police system which was strange to a land which for four hundred years had been subject to Roman influence. Germanic law, unlike that of the Romans, was not a result of governmental legislation, but was made up of customs of the tribe and was generally unwritten. There was no studied effort to sift through the facts of a case as had been done in Roman courts. Instead, an appeal was

[3]John Liversidge, *Britain in the Roman Empire* (New York: Frederick Praeger, Publisher, 1968), p. 295.

[4]*Ibid.,* pp. 295-296.

made to the gods to decide the issue. The burden of proof was on the accused to clear himself, this being done in one of three ways:[5]

> **By compurgation.** The defendant would try to exonerate himself by taking a solemn oath that he did not commit the offense in question. Friends or relatives were often hired as "oath helpers" to aid the accused. The defendant and his "witnesses" were made to recite an exact oath, and if the slightest slip was made in reciting the words, the adjudication was "guilty."
>
> **Trial by ordeal.** In cases where the oath was judged to be insufficient to prove innocence, the accused had to clear himself by undergoing a painful ordeal, such as thrusting his hand into a pot of boiling water to retrieve a small object, or carrying a red-hot poker in his hand for twenty paces. Upon completion of the ordeal, the injured hand was wrapped for three days and if after that time it appeared to be healing properly, then the defendant was found innocent.
>
> **Trial by combat.** In some cases a formal duel was arranged between the defendant and his accuser. Trial by combat was usually reserved for the more affluent, who had their champions fight for them. If a defendant's champion was killed, then the accused was adjudged guilty and he paid a fine.

Eventually, however, the barbaric culture of the Anglo-Saxons fused with the more civilized Latin culture to create a medieval system of law enforcement which was, in many ways, unique. In time, two important principles emerged. First was the conception that wherever the king was present, wrongdoing was particularly serious. No unlawfulness should disturb the king's peace lest the perpetrator "be made to make twofold compensation." Gradually the idea of the special nature of the king's peace was to grow until one need but commit an offense anywhere in the realm to *disturb the peace* of the king. The second conception was that all the king's subjects in some way belonged to him. The king was entitled to special compensation if a free man was killed or injured, for he enjoyed the king's protection. The free man, or *churl,* was the prototype of the yeoman, the free farmer who—within the law and subject only to his duty to his king—was master of his own fate. Much of Anglo-Saxon society was founded on this basis. The practice of trying violators of the law in the name of the Crown is

[5]*Supra* note 2, p. 99.

still alive in England today. It has been passed on to America where men are tried by the state in lieu of individual plaintiffs.[6]

## THE CAPITULARIES OF CHARLEMAGNE

In the eighth century A.D., Charlemagne founded an empire in France which was based on two forces: one material—military supremacy; the other moral—religion. A collection of legislative acts or customs, the *Capitularies of Charlemagne,* were passed in 785 A.D. They were the combined work of people and king, providing penalties for crimes and articulating procedures to be followed by government.in its dealings with the citizenry. Enforcement of the acts rested with feudal lords who ruled geographical entities known as *contes* (counties). In 875 A.D. marshals, forerunners of today's French *gendarmerie,* were created by the king to maintain security.[7]

## ENGLISH INNOVATIONS

During the reign of Alfred the Great (871 A.D.-900 A.D.) England was divided into geographical districts known as shires. A shire was roughly equivalent to a county. Local governing units were also more clearly defined. An area in which ten families lived was called a tithing. Ten tithings were known as a hundred. As population burgeoned, hundreds became parishes. Over the years a number of significant law enforcement institutions were created in England, some of which have remained relatively intact to this day. The following innovations deserve attention.

### The Tithingman

From each tithing a man was chosen to insure that the members of his group obeyed the law. Each person in the tithing was required to give his pledge or surety for the good conduct of himself and other members of the tithing. The system was primarily one of social control and if one member of the group committed a crime, the whole community acted as prosecutors.

[6]Beram Saklatvala, *The Origins of the English People* (New York: Taplinger Publishing Company, 1969), pp. 87-91.

[7]Lucien Romier, *A History of France* (New York: St. Martins Press, 1966), pp. 59-63.

The duties of the tithingman were to raise the hue and cry and to run through the streets informing all that a crime had been committed. This sytem of mutual responsibility was called the mutual pledge system.

### The Shire-Reeve

In order to maintain law and order in the shires, the king appointed a reeve (judge) to act in his behalf. The shire-reeve acted as magistrate and chief law enforcement officer in the county. The term *shire-reeve* was modified over the years until it became *sheriff.* To keep peace within his jurisdiction, the shire-reeve often traveled by horseback to each hundred to hold court and to investigate allegations of wrongdoing.

### The Parish Constable System

As the hundreds grew in size, parishes were created. With this development, the first real law enforcement officer, the constable, was appointed by local noblemen to police the rural parishes and to maintain the weapons and equipment of each hundred. The parish constable was appointed for a one-year term of service.

### The Watch and Ward System

During the reign of Edward I (1272-1307), the first official police agencies were created in England's burgeoning towns. Groups of men were appointed by town guilds to patrol the streets at night, to maintain a fire watch, and to arrest those who committed crimes. They were known as the *watch and ward.*

### Justice of the Peace

In 1326 Edward II created the office of justice of the peace to supplement the mutual pledge system. At first, noblemen were appointed to the position, their primary job being to assist the sheriff in maintaining order in the county. In time, however, the peace justice assumed the role of chief county magistrate in addition to his police function. Because of their noble birth, justices of the peace began to assert leadership over constables. By the end of the fourteenth century the constable served the justice by inquiring into criminal offenses, serving summonses, executing warrants, and taking charge of prisoners. This "essentially set the pattern for the next 500 years. The Justice remained the superior, the constable the inferior, conservator of the peace until the second quarter of the nineteenth century."[8]

## CONCLUSION[9]

Meanwhile, over the years, the local pledge system continued to decline. Community support languished. And with considerable reason. What was everybody's business became nobody's duty, and citizens who were bound by law to take their turn at police work gradually evaded personal police service by paying others to do the work for them. In theory constables were appointed annually, but in fact their work was done by deputies or substitutes who so acted year after year, being paid to do so by the constables. These early paid police officers did not rank high in popular estimation as indicated in contemporary references. They were usually ill-paid and ignorant men, often too old to be in any sense efficient. But, as the local pledge system was declining, innovations were cropping up in the emerging cities of the seventeenth and eighteenth centuries. Those first law enforcement officers were increasingly assisted by a paid night-watch force. Although these nominally were responsible for guarding the cities against thieves and vandals, apparently they were not effective. Reportedly they did little more than roam the streets at night, periodically calling out the condition of the weather, the hour, and the fact that "all was well."

---

[8]Reprinted from The President's Commission on Law Enforcement and Administration of Justice, *Task Force Report: The Police* (Washington: U. S. Government Printing Office, 1967), pp. 3-4.

[9]*Ibid.*, p. 4.

An artist's conception of a public execution in early London.

*Chapter 2*

# IN COLONIAL AMERICA (1608-1783)

**P**uritanism, which dominated the intellectual life of colonial New England for nearly a century after its founding, has been a major force in shaping the American mind. Puritan ideology rested on the assumption that government was necessary because of the sinfulness of man, hence it was essential that government enforce conformity to law—God's law as the Puritans interpreted it. The Puritans established their government on a religious and a civil foundation. They felt that government should be based on the consent of the governed; however, the Puritans defined liberty as the freedom to do what was "just and right." They accepted the existence of a fundamental law that transcended the importance of any human law or edict. In Puritanism, the fundamental law was to be found in the Scriptures. On the idea of a "Bible commonwealth," John Cotton, an early Puritan leader, stated:[1]

> It is very suitable to God's all-sufficient wisdom, and to the fullness and perfection of Holy Scriptures, not only to prescribe perfect rules for the right ordering of a private man's soul to everlasting blessedness with himself, but also for the right ordering of a man's family, yea, of the commonwealth too, so far as both of them are subordinate to spiritual ends. . .

To the Puritans their system left no room for the toleration of "outside" ideas. Activistic, moralistic, even rationalistic, Puritanism developed in different directions on American shores. And, according to leading scholars one of its paths led to political intolerance and the suppression of dissent; another led to a comparatively high intellectual and literary level.[2]

In time, however, the theocracy established by the Puritans began to crumble, partly as a result of internal tensions and partly

---

[1]From Cotton's letter to Lord Saye in 1630, reprinted in Gerald N. Grob and Robert N. Beck, Eds., *American Ideas,* Vol. I (New York: The Free Press, 1963), p. 43.

[2]*Ibid.,* pp. 5-6.

because of environmental factors. Yet, even after the passing of Puritanism, their ideas lingered on, and these ideas can be seen even today in the promulgation of laws and in their enforcement. Prohibition, for example, was a natural outgrowth of Puritan thought. For better and for worse the mark of the Puritan mind has been indelibly stamped on the American scene, and the unfolding history of law enforcement bears that imprint.

## THE EARLY EXPERIENCE

When in the seventeenth century settlers began migrating to the New World, they brought with them the systems of law enforcement, admittedly imperfect, that they had known in Europe. Yet, although the basic structure of the institutions and ideas remained intact for a time, the physical and eventually the cultural environment of America forced modifications in even the most revered and deeply entrenched customs.

### Jamestown and Dale's Laws

The earliest settlers to America's eastern shore were decimated not only by the harsh environment of their strange new surroundings, but by internal descension and petty jealousies. To use the phrase of a later day, the colony suffered from "too many chiefs, and not enough Indians." Practically one half of Jamestown's early settlers were gentlemen accustomed to taking orders from no one, "ten times more fit to spoil a commonwealth than to maintain one."[3] As a result, only thirty-eight of the original one hundred forty-four settlers survived the first year. Jamestown seemed headed for a disastrous fate; however, the arrival of the legendary John Smith saved the day. Smith forced everyone to work, under threat of banishment to the wilderness for slackers. In 1609 a "great fleet" left London bound for Jamestown carrying six hundred men, women, and children. Arriving in time for the severe American winter, the "unbridled multitude" entered into a "starving time" in which people died by the scores. The pioneers of Jamestown survived because of an almost superhuman will to do so and because of a system of law and enforcement initiated by two

---

[3]David Hawke, *The Colonial Experience* (New York: The Bobbs-Merrill Company, Inc., 1966), p. 91.

early leaders, Thomas Gates and Thomas Dale. The law, often referred to as Dale's Laws, but formally titled *Laws Divine, Moral and Martial,* was a mixture of civil and martial law. The legal code was strict as was the enforcement of it. The severity of punishment for seemingly minor infractions emphasized the degree to which the settlers were expected to conform to established procedure. The law was enforced *to the letter!* When in 1612 several colonists attempted to escape from Virginia in stolen boats, the governor had them shot, hanged, and broken on the wheel, according to their degree of involvement. This system was in direct conflict with the English system of justice which the settlers had known, a system which had emphasized human liberty and personal freedom. *Dale's Laws* represented a severe and repressive set of measures, yet, one must keep in mind that the code was promulgated in response to a need, an important element in the total American experience. Had these early laws not been so severe and so rigidly enforced, the whole colony should surely have perished. According to a noted historian:[4]

> If these laws had not been so strictly executed, I see not how the utter subversion of the colony should have been prevented. And for all their harshness, they did give the settlers a government of laws. . .

### The Chesapeake Sheriff

The impetus for settling Maryland came mainly from gentlemen adventurers who dreamed of reproducing in the New World the England they had known. The old English hundred was resurrected as the key local unit. Although the earliest Maryland settlement was considered a military outpost, by 1632 the office of sheriff had been substituted for the provost marshal, the chief military law officer. The *Chesapeake sheriff* resembled closely the English sheriff, with only minor modifications. He was the ranking police and financial officer of each county. He served warrants and made arrests. He collected taxes, ministers' dues, and fees owed the governor; and he received ten percent of all he took in. At first the sheriff was chosen by the county court from among three men recommended by the governor; but by 1645 he was picked from among eight members of the county court, with the post rotating

---

[4]*Ibid.,* p. 97.

annually to a new member. The position served as a financial reward for magistrates, who otherwise went unpaid.

## The Monthly Courts

As the Chesapeake colonies patterned their local governing units after the English model, each county was assigned its own monthly court, staffed by court commissioners, or justices of the peace as they would later be called. The judges, appointed by the governor, were supposed to travel their districts and dispense justice. Officers of the court included sheriffs, constables, clerks, and coroners.

## New Netherlands' Schout Fiscal

When the Dutch West India Company settled New Netherlands (New York), it created the office of *schout fiscal* (sheriff-attorney). Like many of the offices in colonial times, the schout fiscal fulfilled a multitude of assignments. In New Netherlands he was attorney general and sheriff. In this double capacity he saw that all placards, ordinances, military regulations, and commands of the states general (governor) and the company were executed and obeyed. In addition, the schout acted as a check on the excesses of other appointed officials. The first schout fiscal, Hendrick Van Dyck, evidently felt the press of his many duties, as he was dismissed for drunkenness.[5]

## The Military Police

The use of the military in policing civilian communities has a long history in America. In fact, many towns were initially policed by militia units for considerable periods of time. Fort Pontchartrain (Detroit), for example, labored under martial law for the first hundred years of its existence. Law enforcement in New Orleans was handled by the military for eighty-five years before a formal police constabulary was founded. In Cincinnati, soldiers from nearby Fort Washington provided police protection for years. The story was the same in hundreds of other communities.

[5]Herbert L. Osgood, *The American Colonies in the Seventeenth Century* (Gloucester: Peter Smith, 1957), pp. 105-106.

Sometimes, citizen police and the militia worked side by side in bringing law and order to early towns. Even after formal police departments were established, each state chose to retain its militia. The use of militia as a police force is deeply entrenched in the American experience. Throughout history, incidents of collective crime and violence have brought requests from local officials that the militia be dispatched to aid or replace besieged local police units. The habit of relying on the militia to perform needed public safety functions started early in the country and has persisted to this day.

## TOWARD AN AMERICAN SYSTEM OF LAW ENFORCEMENT

A system of American law enforcement was being formed long before the Revolution as colonial administrators adopted and adapted the usages of their European systems to the peculiar jurisdictional scheme and altered social circumstances prevailing in the New World. Cultures met and blended, as did law enforcement methods. The result was a brand of enforcement which resembled Old World institutions but which, in rather substantial ways, was unique. As the early settlements grew in size the problems created by this growth prompted a movement toward comprehensive laws and firm, often rigid, law enforcement. America, even in the seventeenth century, was gaining a reputation for lawlessness, wanton violence, and hedonism, a reputation not entirely unearned, although the English conception of the New World as a hotbed of criminal activity was greatly exaggerated. Yet crime existed and violence occurred regularly enough to be of concern to colonial leaders. It will do well to briefly examine the systems of pre-Revolutionary law enforcement in two early colonial towns: Boston and New York.

### The Boston Watch

On April 12, 1631, the Boston Court ordered that "watches" be set up at sunset, thereby founding the first night watch in America. The watch consisted of six men and an officer and took on the characteristics of a military guard. In 1634 the position of constable was created, with William Chesebrough assuming the post. On February 27, 1636, a town watch was created that differed from the early watch in that it was staffed by citizens—

not soldiers—who were appointed by the town government. The town watch, except for a brief time during the Revolution, was to persist in one form or another for almost two hundred years. It was not until 1712, however, that Boston voted to pay watchmen for their toil. Boston's early laws were numerous and the punishment for violations was often extreme. Some examples:

**1639.** Edward Palmer, a carpenter, was commissioned to build stocks (a device in which criminals were set for punishment) for the City of Boston. When finished, he presented his bill to city officials, who thought it to be exorbitant and proceeded to fine him five pounds and lock him in his own device.

**1649.** Margaret Jones was hanged for witchcraft when it was reported that "a little child was seen to run from her."

**1650.** The wearing of "great boots" and other such extravagant articles of dress was forbidden unless the wearer was worth two hundred pounds. That same year, Oliver Holmes was whipped "for being a Baptist."

In 1652, in response to a series of accidental fires, the watch was supplied with bells to sound the alarm. Their tour of duty was modified to a seven-hour shift—ten P.M. to five A.M. In 1701 the watch was directed to patrol silently—without bells—from "ten o'clock till broad daylight." In 1735 watchmen were "ordered to cry the time of night and state of the weather, in a moderate tone, as they walk their rounds after twelve o'clock." Few significant changes in the structure of Boston law enforcement occurred until after the Revolution.[6]

## Changes in New York

As the population of New Netherlands burgeoned, the Dutch government established a burgher watch in 1643 to assist the schout fiscal in enforcing the few laws that had been promulgated. In an effort to motivate citizens to obey the law, a gibbet, or whipping post, was installed on the waterfront, on which violators were spread-eagled, beaten, and displayed for all to see.

In 1652 the flourishing settlement on Manhatten Island was incorporated and named Nieuw Amsterdam (New York City).

[6]Edward H. Savage, *Police Records and Recollections* (Boston: John P. Dale & Company, 1873), pp. 5-26.

That same year a *rattel wacht* (rattle watch) was formed, made up of citizens equipped with rattles for summoning assistance. The watch was a sentinel-type organization assigned to fixed posts. In 1658 the first police force worthy of the name was established when eight *paid* watchmen were appointed to replace the citizen volunteers.

When in 1664 the British took over Nieuw Amsterdam, the Dutch and English cultures blended and the police force underwent minor modification. The police of the city, now known as New York, were placed under the command of a high constable, Obe Hendrick by name. Law enforcement remained relatively static for the next several decades. In 1693 the first uniformed officer was appointed, as the mayor, Isaac De Reimer, selected a twelve-man watch to secure the city, which now numbered five thousand. The first precinct station, called a watch house, was constructed in 1731, the same year a stage line was initiated from Boston to New York.

### CRIMINAL JUSTICE IN THE COLONIES

To be accused of a crime in colonial America, regardless of the nature of the offense, was a traumatic experience even for the innocent. For the burden of proof rested not with the accuser, but with the accused. Accounts of crime in newspapers and history books indicate that accusation was tantamount to conviction, if not in a court of law then in the court of public opinion, and conviction always meant punishment of some sort, punishment that was often physically painful. Early laws banned not only traditional antisocial behavior—murder, rape, robbery, theft, etc.—but "offensive behavior," such as gossiping, name calling, mockery, and taunting. Colonial courtrooms overflowed with complainants anxious to file charges of libel or petty slander against neighbors, debtors, or even members of their own families. More often than not a whispered slander led to a trial, a conviction, and public punishment, all in the same day. Punishment was purposely harsh, as colonial officials wished to deter future crime. The rate of recidivism must have been low, for few people could survive more than one or two brushes with colonial criminal justice. In each community certain devices were installed for use by the courts in punishing offenders. Some of the more common

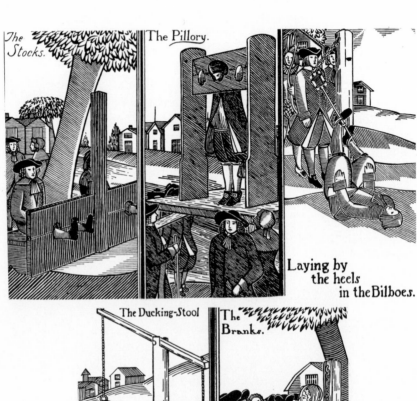

The end result of criminal justice in Colonial America often meant punishment by simple, yet effective, devices. *(Courtesy of Patterson Smith Publishing Corp.)*

apparatuses used were the following:[7]

**The Bilboes.** This device consisted of a long iron bar with two shackles, not unlike handcuffs, into which an offender's legs were locked. The bar prevented the prisoner from moving. It was not unusual for an offender to be sentenced to two days in the bilboes for "swearynge."

**The Ducking Stool.** The ducking stool was an armchair fastened to the end of two beams and and placed at the edge of a pond or river. Offenders were strapped into the chair and plunged into the water as often as the sentence directed. Dunking was the most ignoble form of early punishment; it was usually reserved for gossiping housewives and drunken sailors.

**The Stocks.** In New England the first public building erected in a new community was a meeting house; however, before even it was built, a pair of stocks was installed. Stocks were simply low wooden benches with leg-holes, in which prisoners were secured. It was the duty of citizens to pass by the unfortunate prisoner and reproach him for his sins.

**The Pillory.** The pillory, or "stretch-neck" as it was called, was an upright hinged board with a hole in which a person's head was set fast. During the early use of the device, prisoners' ears were nailed to either side of the head-hole and they were made to stand in an upright position for hours. A farmer who plowed his field on a holy day, and was caught, could expect to spend his next work day in the pillory.

**The Brank.** The brank, or "scolds bridle," was an iron cage of great weight which covered the entire head. Often a flat tongue of iron was placed in the prisoner's mouth to prevent conversation. The brank was an English invention which did not achieve popularity in the New World. It was generally reserved for "paupers, blasphemers, and insubordinate wives."

## LYNCH LAW

In backwoods areas, where no formal criminal justice systems existed, citizens were often tempted to take the law into their own

---

[7]Alice Morse Earle, *Curious Punishments of Bygone Days* (Montclair, New Jersey: Patterson Smith Publishing Corp. Originally published in 1896, reprinted in 1969).

hands. Most resisted the temptation, but some did not. Where the power of the civil government had not been fully established, persons would band together to mete out "justice" to those individuals who had transgressed on the peace, safety, or property of another. This private administration of justice was termed *lynching* or *lynch law* after its American originator, who many believe was Charles Lynch, a Virginia farmer who at the time of the Revolution headed a small band of men who tracked down and punished desperadoes, outlaws, wayward Indians, and British sympathizers.

Lynching was not an American phenomenon. It had been used in medieval Germany, in Spain, and even in seventeenth-century England. But the frequency with which Americans used it, together with the incredibly long period of time it persisted in certain sections of the country—notably the West and the South-east—gave it a distinctly American flavor. As time went on, lynchings began to take the form of hangings as America's burgeoning population and its ever expanding frontier created the need for some type of law enforcement, formal or otherwise. If lynching proved anything, it was that there was a dramatic need for formal, professional law enforcement systems which negated the need for extralegal collective citizen violence.

## DEVELOPMENTS IN ENGLAND

By the end of the seventeenth century, the English parish-constable system began to break down, partly because of the crush of population—London alone had approximately 500,000 inhabitants—and partly because of an alarmingly high crime rate. A system of night watchmen had been established in the reign of Charles II; however, watchmen were generally old and feeble citizens who "paraded the streets at night with a lantern, loudly proclaiming their presence by shouting the hours and announcing the state of the weather."[8]

Deputy-constables were found to be little more than professional criminals who worked, for a price, in close cooperation with thieves, vice-purveyors, and lawbreakers of every variety.

---

[8]Charles Reith, *A Short History of the British Police* (London: Oxford University Press, 1948), pp. 5-6.

London's growing trade and industry added to the problem by attracting to the city drifters and rogues from the countryside. Seeing the need for reform, King George in 1737 initiated action to allow city councils to levy taxes to pay nightwatchmen. Thus, *for the first time, tax money was used to pay police salaries.*

In 1748 novelist Henry Fielding was appointed magistrate for Westminster and Middlesex, thanks in no small measure to influential friends who hoped to relieve him of long-standing poverty. Fielding, however tainted his appointment, was a smashing success at his job. He initiated the idea that citizens should band together to *prevent crime,* rather than resisting it individually or waiting for authority to repress it. This concept was to be developed into "the new science of preventive police."* Fielding organized a small group of volunteers to police the crime-ridden Bow Street neighborhood. Remarkably, crime was checked. The volunteer patrols, made up of male householders, were eventually paid for their services and, in time, became the Bow Street Runners and Patrols. A mobile group who moved swiftly to the scenes of crimes to begin immediate investigations, the Bow Street Runners were the first police detective units.

*A term coined by Scottish social reformer Patrick Colquhoun, who founded the Thames River Police.

Sir Robert Peel, British Home Secretary, who in 1829 submitted to Parliament the Metropolitan Police Bill, a legislative enactment of enormous importance in the evolution of law enforcement.

*Chapter 3*

# LAW ENFORCEMENT IN THE
# POST-REVOLUTION PERIOD (1784-1829)

$T$he American Revolution rudely interrupted the trend toward formal civilian law enforcement as troops—either English or American, depending on which was the occupying force—took over the public safety duties previously performed by civilians. In most cases the conflict resulted in the suspension of jury trials and the replacement of civil magistrates by military tribunals. The military primarily concerned itself with defense against external attack and, as a consequence, petty crimes were often ignored and vice was allowed to flourish Protection against internal disorder was of little concern to the Army, and only cursory attention was paid to citizens' demands for police protection. Furthermore, the military itself contributed to the crime problem, wartime soldiers being a rather raucous lot. After the Revolution, however, civilian governmental control was resumed and life in America approached a state of near normalcy. On September 9, 1787, a court in Boston passed the following sentences: "One burglar to be hung; five female thieves to be whipped; four males thieves whipped; two big thieves to sit on the gallows; one counterfeiter to stand in pillory and have the right ear cut off. . ."[1]

Indeed things *were* returning to normal.

Although the end of the Revolution returned law enforcement to civilian control, it also aggravated the crime problem. Many upper-class Loyalists had left the country during the English evacuation and, as a result, an important component of social control was removed from communities badly in need of a stabilizing influence. Furthermore, the economic life of the young nation had suffered greatly during the war, prompting crimes

---

[1]Edward H. Savage, *Police Records and Recollections* (Boston: John P. Dale and Company, 1873), p. 41.

against persons to rise dramatically. Thieves and desperadoes had little trouble evading capture as war-damaged areas, of which most communities had their share, were converted into sanctuaries for rogues. Each community had a name for these shanty towns—in New York City it was Canvas Town. Civil policemen were reluctant to enter these areas unless accompanied by the militia. Not surprisingly, crime and vice thrived.

Toward the end of the eighteenth century law enforcement in the cities was still a rather haphazard undertaking as watchmen walked their rounds shouting out useless information while crimes were perpetrated within plain view. Some communities attempted to deal with the rising incidents of crime and violence by enlarging their police forces and creating specialized crime units; however, although some minor modifications were made in the system of policing, few major structural changes occurred in the post-Revolution period. In 1785 Boston appointed Captain John Ballard, William Billings, and Christopher Clarke as inspectors of police—the first in America.[2] By the end of the eighteenth century the responsibility for policing New York City was divided among five classes of police officers, none of whom wore uniforms:[3]

**The Mayor.** The mayor was the city's chief law enforcement officer who supervised the overall police operation and took charge at fires, riots, and major breaches of the peace.

**The High Constable.** The constable was the mayor's chief assistant. Under law he was required to enforce all state laws and city ordinances. One of the earliest high constables was Jacob Hays, a highly respected officer who had a talent for dealing single-handedly with large mobs without resorting to force.

**Constables.** By the close of the eighteenth century, New York City had sixteen constables. Constables executed arrest warrants, quelled riots, and maintained order. They were elected annually and worked on commission. The more arrests made by a constable, the higher his remuneration.

**Marshals.** The city's forty marshals were appointed by the

---

[2]*Ibid.*

[3]James F. Richardson, *The New York Police* (New York: Oxford University Press, 1970), pp. 16-19.

mayor and held office at his pleasure. Marshals had basically the same responsibilities as constables, their primary duty being to "bring criminals to justice." Marshals were also paid according to the revenue they generated.

**Watchmen.** Watchmen patrolled the city during the hours of darkness. They did not possess police powers and could arrest only if a crime was committed in their physical presence. Watchmen were compensated on a per diem basis. By the turn of the century there were seventy-two watchmen, a figure that increased sevenfold within twenty years.

In 1789 Congress created the first federal enforcement officer in the person of the United States marshal.[4] That same year Congress provided for a Supreme Court of six members by passing the Judiciary Act of 1789, a move which was not to have its full impact on law enforcement for over 150 years.[5] In 1829 the Postal Act was passed and police powers were conferred on a federal agency. Postal inspectors were later appointed to enforce the postal laws.[6]

In 1801 Boston became the first United States city to require by statute the maintenance of a permanent night watch. Boston had little trouble finding applicants for the job because of the generous pay: fifty cents per night. On March 10, 1807, the first police districts were established. On June 16, 1823, Boston appointed its first marshal, James Pollard, a Harvard graduate and a practicing attorney.[7]

Young America was growing by leaps and bounds and communities which had previously relied on the militia for police protection soon found it necessary to create civil police forces. In 1797 Providence hired twelve night watchmen to assume the job formerly held by volunteers and the militia. The men wore no

---

[4]John L. Sullivan, *Introduction to Police Science* (New York: McGraw-Hill, Inc., 1966), p. 150.

[5]Richard T. Current, T. Harry Williams, and Frank Freidel, *American History: A Survey* (New York: Alfred A. Knopf, 1964), p. 131.

[6]*Supra* note 4, p. 150.

[7]Roger Lane, *Policing the City—Boston: 1822-1885* (Cambridge: Harvard University Press, 1967), p. 11.

uniforms, save a cloak, and carried a curved staff as a weapon and for identification purposes. In 1801 the first civilian police officers were appointed in Detroit. Three years later a mobile patrol and a night watch were created. In 1802 Cincinnati, with a population of 800 persons, was incorporated as a town. It had been an unincorporated frontier community since 1788, under the protection of soldiers. Provision was made for the yearly election of a marshal, but in 1803 a disastrous fire prompted the city council to provide for a night watch. All male citizens over the age of twenty-one years were required to serve in rotation without pay. Each night twelve men reported to the watch house where they chose an "officer of the night" who divided them into two classes of six men each to patrol the streets. They were equipped with a rattle for summoning aid, and a lantern. In 1803 the military police passed out of existence in New Orleans and a municipal force was commissioned. Mayor Etienne De Bore appointed a committee of city councilmen to inspect prisons and formulate rules and regulations regarding the police function. Having adopted the regulations in special session, the mayor and his council appointed twenty-five men to carry out the duties of a "police force." A year later the "patrol militia," a civilian patrol unit, was established and in 1806 the *Garde de ville* (city watch) was created. Later that year, however, the grand jury arraigned the force as "inefficient" and it was disbanded. In 1818 money was appropriated to pay watchmen for their services and a professional force consisting of a captain and six watchmen was hired.

The post-Revolutionary War period saw great strides in the improvement of the country's transportation system. Roads and waterways began connecting all parts of the country. In 1807 Robert Fulton's famous steamboat voyage from New York to Albany created a new chapter in communication. Between 1789 and 1810 the total tonnage of American vessels engaged in overseas traffic rose from 125,000 to 1,000,000. In 1818 the turnpike era was well underway as most major cities were connected by new or rebuilt roadways.[8] Great industrial and port cities were emerging and American law enforcement, which was using seventeenth-century police methods to deal with nineteenth-century

[8]*Supra* note 5, pp. 172-173.

problems, was in no position to meet the challenge of crime created by the changes in the nation's social life. Crime and its effects were becoming a way of life to city dwellers. To compound citizens' worry over crime and violence, the American press of the era seemed to devote an inordinate amount of space to crime news, especially sensational street crimes. Fisher Ames, a noted writer of the era, lamented: [9]

> Some of the shocking articles in the paper raise simple, and very simple, wonder; some terrour; and some horror and disgust. Now what institution is there in these endless wonders?...do they not shock tender minds and addle shallow brains? They make a thousand old maids, and eight thousand booby boys afraid to go to bed'' alone...yet there seems to be a rivalship among printers, who shall have the most wonders, and the strangest and most wonderful crimes.

Yet the propensity of the press to gather and print eye-witness accounts of crime notwithstanding, the rate of serious crimes did seem to be rising alarmingly. When in 1812 America again went to war with England, selective mob action created concern among the people for their safety.

## DEVELOPMENTS IN ENGLAND

English police reformers were busily at work in early nine-teenth-century England, although they often met with resistance from a suspicious citizenry and politicians and merchants interested in the financial exploitation of crime. Patrick Colquohoun, magistrate, author, and noted police scholar, published books and pamphlets in which he propounded the principle of *preventing* crime and disorder, an idea he readily acknowledged was inspired by Henry Fielding's Bow Street Runners.[10] Colquohoun's attempts to implement the idea failed because of his inability to overcome much of the prejudice which existed against any formal police unit. He died in 1820, a bitter and defeated man.

Yet, even though Colquohoun's plan met with failure, it was clear that something had to be done to bring law and order to

---

[9]Frank Luther Mott, *The News in America* (Cambridge: Harvard University Press, 1952), p. 50.

[10]Charles Reith, *A New Study of Police History* (London: Oliver and Boyd, 1956), p. 27.

England. Highwaymen and thieves openly pursued their calling, even boasting of successful exploits in inns and eating places. People dared not walk the streets of London after dark unless they were armed. The houses of citizens resembled armed fortresses. In 1822 Sir Robert Peel took office as Home Secretary and attempted to persuade Parliament of the need for a professional police department. Like Colquohoun, he was rebuffed. Peel, however, was not a man to surrender easily. It took him seven years to muster enough political strength to pass his proposal. In 1829 Peel submitted the Metropolitan Police Bill to Parliament, which after much heated debate, passed it, thus enacting the most significant piece of police legislation in history. On September 29, 1829, formal policing began in London as 1,000 men in six divisions began patrolling the streets.

Peelian reform, as it was popularly called, did not meet with the immediate approval of the citizens of London. In fact, many condemned the plan as dangerous and provocative. But, eventually, Peelian reform received widespread acceptance, and the policemen, who were at first sneeringly referred to as "blue devils," became known affectionately as "bobbies" after Peel. The basic tenets of *Peelian reform* were as follows:[11]

1. The police must be stable, efficient, and organized along military lines.
2. The police must be under government control.
3. The absence of crime will best prove the efficiency of police.
4. The distribution of crime news is essential.
5. The deployment of police strength both by time and area is essential.
6. No quality is more indispensable to a policeman than a perfect command of temper; a quiet, determined manner has more effect than violent action.
7. Good appearance commands respect.
8. The securing and training of proper persons is at the root of efficiency.
9. Public security demands that every police officer be given a number.
10. Police headquarters should be centrally located and easily accessible to the people.

[11]A.C. Germann, Frank D. Day, and Robert R.J. Gallati, *Introduction to Law Enforcement and Criminal Justice* (Springfield: Charles C Thomas, Publisher, 1970), p. 54.

11. Policemen should be hired on a probationary basis.
12. Police records are necessary to the correct distribution of police strength.

The first commissioners of police were Colonel Charles Rowan and Richard Mayne. The new police "office" was in a house at 4 Whitehall Place, the rear of which opened onto a courtyard known as Scotland Yard, a name derived from the fact that it had formerly been the residence of ambassadors from the kings of Scotland.

Although Peelian reform had no immediate effect on the United States, it was to later serve as a model for all police departments desirous of creating a professional police force. Peelian reform marked the birth of modern policing. Its impact is still felt in this country and abroad.

### CONCLUSION

America was moving forward as a center of commerce and trade. Cities were evolving and the social dislocation caused by structural changes in the fabric of the new nation created predictable police problems. Although England experienced many of the same problems, its solution—the Metropolitan Police Force—could not be used to the same effect in America. In England the people were used to centralized governmental control; however, Americans had a healthy suspicion of a strong central government, and to even suggest a single unified police force might have led to another revolution. As a result, the country's law enforcement agencies muddled through the period, fragmented and decentralized. There was a lag between the general progress of the country and the ability of the police to cope with the everyday problems created by that progress. The lag threatened to become a chasm in the coming era, a period in which many of the internal national conflicts which had been submerged came bursting to the surface.

Edward H. Savage, Boston Chief of Police (1870-1878), an exceptionally able and humane man, was the first great American police administrator.

*Chapter 4*

# THE GROWTH OF URBAN POLICE SYSTEMS
# (1830-1865)

**A**s American towns burgeoned in population during the first third of the nineteenth century the "traditional police"— sheriffs, constables, marshals, night watchmen, citizen volunteers— were unable to cope with the increasing crime and tumult caused by economic depressions, political upheavals, and a country in transition. Governments' initial response to widespread crime and violence was to increase in numbers the watch and ward; however, it was soon clear to even the most backward public officials that what was needed was a complete restructuring of the system of town law enforcement. The antiquated watch-and-ward system was simply inadequate to handle the problems of the day. When large-scale rioting began plaguing urban areas, it became obvious that towns would have to create a new class of permanent professional police officers to meet the challenge. Reform in the police system came first in communities which experienced extreme criminal violence and rioting.[1] In the face of such difficulties, police machinery went utterly to pieces.

## CRIME, RIOTS, AND A NEW POLICE

Although crime and violence existed in colonial America, it was tolerated by citizens because it usually consisted of petty vice, drunken assaults, and aimless brawls which were dangerous largely to the participants and not to honest citizens. In fact, small riots were often looked on as sporting events. As the press of population began to become a factor in towns, this early tolerance eroded when the scope and intensity of antisocial behavior exploded into crime waves, routs, tumultuous assemblies, and

---

[1]The National Commission on the Causes and Prevention of Violence, *Violence in America* (New York: Signet Books, 1969), p. 56.

dangerous riots.

The nineteenth century saw the beginning of what, unhappily, has become an American tragedy, not to mention a challenge for the nation's lawmen: the bizarre murder case. Tinged with overtones of sex, the phenomenon of grisly homicides made their ugly mark on the national scene. With the pyrotechnic entry of the penny press, the normal pressure on the police to solve gruesome murders became even greater as the fledgling newspaper industry sensationalized every case to the horrified delight of a fascinated public. Three cases typified the era's homicidal fare:[2]

**The Robinson-Jewett Case.** In Philadelphia in 1836 a prostitute, Helen Jewett, was found brutally murdered in her room. A young clerk by the name of Robinson was arrested and charged with the crime by a police force which had been pressured by the press into a premature arrest. Robinson was tried, but during the course of his trial, evidence was presented that exonerated the defendant, thereby prompting editorial barbs at the police, the court, and the jury.

**The Webster Case.** In 1849 the dismembered parts of Dr. George Parkman's body were found in the laboratory of a Harvard chemistry professor named John W. Webster, a creditor of Parkman's. Webster was tried and convicted of murder and sentenced to die on the gallows. At his execution a mob of persons rioted when they were unable to get a better view of the hanging. Two hundred and fifty people were admitted as witnesses, many of whom were policemen.

**The Sickles Case.** In 1859 Daniel E. Sickles shot and killed Phillip Barton Key, United States Attorney for the District of Columbia, for seducing his wife. Sickles, a member of the United States House of Representatives, was arrested and tried for the murder. The newspapers gave the trial front page treatment. Sickles, an obviously guilty man, was acquitted by a jury which granted that special leniency was reserved for outraged husbands who strike down rival lovers.

Publicized crimes of the day, coupled with extreme collective violence, indicated to citizens that cities needed to be secured, and public officials moved to secure them by implementing urban police systems.

---

[2]John Lofton, *Justice and the Press* (Boston: Beacon Press, 1966), pp. 74-75.

## Philanthrophy and the Police: The Philadelphia Story

Philadelphia's problems with crime, violence, and vice were not unique, but the impetus for creating a day police force in that city was. In 1833 Stephen Girard, a wealthy philanthropist, died and bequeathed a large sum of money to the city of Philadelphia for the financing of a "competent police." The intent of the generous but peculiar bequest was as follows:[3]

> To enable the corporation of the City of Philadelphia to provide more effectually than they now do for the security and property of the persons and property of the inhabitants of the said city by a competent police, including a sufficient number of watchmen really suited to the purpose; and to this end I recommend a division of the city into watch districts of four parts, each under a proper head; and that at least two watchmen shall in each round or station patrol together.

The will either stimulated or shamed the city into action and later that year an ordinance was passed providing for a day force of twenty-four policemen as well as 120 night watchmen. Girard's simple but innovative recommendations were followed, and some equally precedent-setting ideas of the mayor were incorporated into the ordinance, which centralized control of the new force in a single head known as a captain, who was appointed by the mayor. Vacancies in higher ranks were to be filled by promoting those who "have distinguished themselves by diligence, integrity, and skill in an inferior grade," thus lessening political influences over the force. The new force proved successful; though within two years, partly because of politics and partly because of economics, the ordinance was repealed and the previous system was resurrected.[4]

It became clear almost immediately that the old way of policing the city was inadequate. The defects in the system were dramatically underscored when, in 1838, Negro rioting exploded in Philadelphia. Scores were killed and historic Pennsylvania Hall was burned. In 1842 riots again broke out and hundreds of churches, meeting places, and homes were burned. In 1848 Philadelphia re-established an independent day force, consisting of thirty-four

---

[3]Raymond B. Fosdick, *American Police Systems* (New York: The Century Co., 1921), pp. 63-64.

[4]*Ibid.*, p. 69.

policemen. The old night watch remained in its original form. Six years later, in 1854, the day and night forces were consolidated and placed under a marshal, popularly elected every two years.

## Boston's Police: Problems and Opportunities

Boston's time of tumult began on August 11, 1834, when a hostile crowd, led by a gang known as the Boston Truckmen, routed nuns from Mount Benedict Convent and burned the structure to the ground.[5] A second major disturbance occurred when the controversial editor, William Lloyd Garrison, was assaulted in the office of *The Liberator* by a crowd infuriated by his anti-slavery writings.[6] On June 11, 1837, the Broad Street Riot occurred when volunteer firemen engaged in a bloody clash with an Irish funeral procession. The conflict was a result of the smoldering resentment toward immigrants, and it marked the first time in Boston's history that the militia had to be called out to quell a disturbance.[7] On April 15, 1838, the General Court of Massachusetts passed a bill creating a permanent day police force to supplement its night watch. By June, nine policemen "with all but the civil powers of constables," were assigned to "whatever duties the council might require."[8] The new police worked so well that in 1839 the elated mayor of Boston, Samuel A. Eliot, declared that "the public peace has been uninterrupted during the past year, and. . .the reputation of the city has suffered no such blow as was inflicted on it in previous years."[9] Although the new police were working well, the city experienced trouble in finding a competent marshal to run the force. Finally, the sixth marshal in a decade, Francis Tukey, was appointed in 1846. Marshal Tukey, only thirty-two years old, was one of America's first legendary law enforcement officers. Taking control of the police department, which had now grown to thirty-eight, Tukey created a competent

---

[5] James McKellar Bugbee, "Boston Under the Mayors: 1822-1880," *The Memorial History of Boston*, Ed. Justin Winsor (Boston: 1881), Vol. III, Ch. II, pp. 238-240.

[6] Roger Lane, *Policing the City—Boston: 1822-1885* (Cambridge: Harvard University Press, 1967), pp. 31-32.

[7] *Supra* note 5, pp. 243-246.

[8] *Supra* note 6, p. 37.

[9] *Ibid.*, p. 39.

and efficient force and built a reputation for himself as a "tough cop." When he expanded his night police force to twenty-two, it captured more criminals than the entire rival body of over two hundred night watchmen. It also served to antagonize much of the public and the city's politicians. Marshal Tukey initiated a *show up,* a weekly roundup of rogues and cutthroats who were paraded before the entire police force. In 1853 Tukey was charged with malfeasance in office and replaced, thus ending an unforgettable era in the history of Boston law enforcement. The years that followed saw a dramatic transformation of police operations: police divisions were created and eight precinct stations were opened and staffed; the city created the country's first detective division in 1851 and followed it by organizing the first harbor patrol in 1853. On May 19, 1855, the separate Boston watch and police were reorganized into the Boston Police Department. The Civil War years were marked by urban disruptions, including a major draft riot, which severely tested the mettle of the new Boston Police Department, and a major police scandal that rocked the very foundation of the department. The Boston Police Department not only survived but grew and prospered. When in 1870 Boston's aldermen fired their chief of police, the entire command structure of the police department—to its everlasting credit— nominated one of its own as a replacement. The board followed the recommendation and Edward Hartwell Savage, an impeccably honest and humane man, was appointed. Many men were to become distinguished, reform-minded American police administrators in the upcoming decades; Savage, however, was the first. Chief Savage remained in office for eight years, during which he was to effect substantial internal reforms. The crime rate was significantly lowered. Incidents of public drunkenness and affray were lessened. Officers' pay was raised, manpower was deployed on a more equitable basis, and the chief became a moral force for community change. Under Chief Savage's administration "there were no dramatic incidents, scandals, or investigations. . . The principle of law enforcement was accepted, while the pacification of the city was measured by declining rates of intemperance and of homicide, and by the passing of riot as a normal form of political expression."[10]

---

[10]*Supra* note 6, p. 178.

## New York's Model Police

By 1844 the population of New York City had risen to 550,000, while the police force numbered 1,000. The force consisted of three distinct components: the police proper, known as Harper's Police, after the mayor; the municipal police; and the night watch, who were compensated at the rate of one dollar and twenty-five cents per night. Recognizing the difficulties involved in maintaining three separate police units, the New York legislature abolished its night watch and implemented a combined day and night police force. Thus, New York City became the first American community to create a unified police department. The force was fashioned after Sir Robert Peel's bobbies, the London Metropolitan Police Department. The next year, eight-pointed copper stars were issued to officers for purposes of identification. New York City's first Chief of Police was also appointed that year. All was not rosy for New York law enforcement, however. The composition of the police force was predominately Irish, provoking deep antagonisms in the community. In 1855 Chief of Police Matsell was accused of "Irishizing" his force, a charge he denied. The city's face was rapidly changing and vicious gang fights became commonplace. In 1851 jealousy between the followers of two popular stage actors erupted into the Astor Place Riots, in which scores of people were killed. Gangs such as The Bowery Boys and The Dead Rabbits terrorized citizens, with little interference from the police. New York's melting pot had not yet reached a boil, and racial and ethnic tensions were at fever pitch.

## The Idea Spreads

Other communities soon followed the lead of Philadelphia, Boston, and New York in establishing urban police forces. In 1842 Cincinnati appointed a paid day police force of two men to supplement its night watch. By 1855 the day force had grown to one hundred men, three of whom were detectives. The following year uniforms of a sort were issued to each man. In 1859 Detroit inaugerated a merchant's police to patrol the downtown commercial area. By 1866 the force was enlarged to fifty-one men, and a detective bureau was formed. Two years later a sanitary unit was created to assist the Board of Health.

## THE CONTROVERSY OVER UNIFORMS

Police in the middle nineteenth century were characterized by their ragtag dress and undisciplined appearance. It was not unusual for officers on the same police force to be dressed in an entirely different fashion. The summer uniform in most cities consisted of white duck suits, except for those officers who did not own a suit, in which case it was short-sleeved shirt, color unspecified, and baggy trousers. In 1853 J. W. Gerard, a noted journalist of the time, wrote a description of the New York Police:

> If you want one suddenly by night or by day, where will you look for him?. . .look at their style of dress, some with hats, some with caps, some with coats like Joseph's of old, parti-colored. If they were mustered together they would look like Falstaff's Regiment.

In response to increasing criticism of police slovenliness, officials in major cities began to provide their forces with uniforms, thereby igniting another controversy among citizens and policemen as well. Many policemen fought the adoption of uniforms vigorously, maintaining, at least privately, that the job was dangerous enough without advertising that one was an officer. Furthermore, uniforms would hinder many extracurricular

Police uniforms in the pre-Civil War era resembled gentlemen's livery, as illustrated above by the policemen of the City of Boston. From left to right: captain, patrolman, deputy chief, chief, lieutenant, and patrolman.

activities such as drinking and sleeping on duty. Citizen opposition to police uniforms was as emotional as officers' resistance was pragmatic. The basis of opposition was an American suspicion of all forms of militarism. Some writers blasted the idea as being "un-American" and "un-democratic"; "an imitation of royalty." Community leaders sneered at the "poppinjays" governments would create with the new livery. Statutes proposing uniformed police forces were consistently voted down by legislators who feared antagonizing the citizenry and angering policemen. Some police departments were persuaded to adopt regulation caps, though the headgear was often stuffed into a handy pocket when an officer patrolled his beat. Even attempts to force policemen to wear badges met with bitter opposition. It was not until 1861 that

Detroit's "Flying Squad" sped to the scene of crimes in progress and tumultuous assemblies, relying on its trusty two-horsepower vehicle. During the Civil War the controversy over police uniforms was resolved as policemen adopted uniforms strikingly similar to Union Army livery. *(Courtesy of the Detroit Police Department)*

uniforms received the full approval of American citizens. In that year the Civil War erased any stigma attached to a uniform.[11]

## POLICE PERSONNEL: A CRISIS OF CONFIDENCE

Conditions in American cities during the era cried out for the strong hand of a well-organized police. But, with few exceptions, it was a cry unanswered, as most forces overlooked the most fundamental kind of reform: the need for competent line personnel. Journalists often complained that the police "inspired no respect." Newspaper stories abounded with tales of policemen actually fleeing from the scene of trouble. Gangs set upon and beat patrolmen for sport. Adding to the negative police image was the insistence of some officers to place themselves above the law they had sworn to enforce. In 1852 the New York Board of Aldermen released a report which documented the areas of police misconduct. The Board charged that:

> Assaulting superior officers, refusing to go on patrol, releasing prisoners from the custody of other policemen, drunkenness, extorting money from prisoners—these were offenses of daily occurrence, committed often with impunity under the protection of a political overlord.

To say, as did one Presidential commission, that "the police mission in the mid-1800s precluded any brilliance," was an understatement. But what could young America expect? Officers were badly paid, untrained, and ill-equipped. They often labored under the domineering influence of corrupt politicians in communities that were seemingly oblivious to their plight. It was little wonder that the quality of personnel attracted to the police craft was generally low. Yet, with all the negative aspects of the dangerous and dirty task, a dedicated group of young men still chose to pursue careers as policemen. And this has become a recurring historical phenomenon. No matter how many corrupting influences infiltrated a police department, regardless of how many officers went bad, there was always a group in that department, sometimes a small one, which resisted the temptations and remained impeccably honest and fair-minded in the face of tremendous obstacles.

[11]Howard O. Sprogle, *The Philadelphia Police: Past and Present* (Philadelphia: 1887), p. 123.

## EARLY METHODS OF POLICE ADMINISTRATION

In colonial days, police executives were chosen in a rather haphazard fashion: some were popularly elected for varying terms of office; others were appointed by mayors, councilmen, or governors; still others simply assumed posts no one else wanted. But as the country grew in size and the problems of policing became more pronounced, citizens and public officials began to realize that new methods were needed to oversee city police operations. The very creation of an executive head—a marshal or chief—was a dramatic step forward; but it was only *one* step. Complicating the search for a method was the "spoils system," a phenomenon that made even the best methods suspect in the eyes of the public. Police departments in cities were often totally in the hands of the politicians in power. Early negative reaction to this system of political domination resulted in the establishment of partisan administrative boards to run police departments.

### Partisan Administrative Boards

In the middle nineteenth century, many city governments lodged the power to oversee police operations in the hands of administrative boards staffed by judges, politicians, businessmen, and private citizens.[12] The plan was hailed by many as an impressive reform in police management and hundreds of towns and cities experimented with the concept, including New York City, Cincinnati, New Orleans, and Omaha. But the system of multiple control soon proved faulty. The boards, whether appointed or elected, were partisan in nature, meaning that they still reflected the views of the political party in power. Accordingly, "both police management and police protection continued to flounder in political uncertainty, intrigue, partisanship, and corruption."[13] Police corruption became a national issue, and state legislatures, dominated by rural politicians who used any opportunity to stifle urban political bosses, were quick to strike by enacting statutes

[12]International City Managers' Association, *Municipal Police Administration,* 5th ed. (Washington: International City Managers' Association, 1961), p. 43.

[13]*Ibid.*

which swept away local control of the police, substituting in its place a system of state control.

## State Control of the Police

Like many police reforms, the system of state control began in New York City when in 1857 the state legislature ruled that New York City was too corrupt to govern itself and seized control of the New York Police Department, arousing bitter resentment from politicians and citizens who held mass meetings, engaged in violent demonstrations, and even instituted court suits to protest the action. The legislature passed the Metropolitan Police Bill which was modeled after Sir Robert Peel's London Metropolitan Police Bill of 1829. The police force was to be regulated by a board appointed by the governor. When the state tried to implement the new law, New York City's mayor, Fernando Wood, defiantly formed a police force loyal to him. For a time two complete sets of policemen patrolled the streets of New York City. Clashes were

A police riot. For a time in 1857 two separate and distinct police forces patrolled the City of New York: one was controlled by the city; the other was a state-appointed force named the Metropolitan Police but popularly referred to as "the Mets." A series of clashes occurred between the two rival forces *(depicted above),* but in the end the state force prevailed as the Mets won the series. *(Courtesy of the Patterson Smith Publishing Corp.)*

frequent and, in one bizzare incident, hundreds of club-swinging policemen from both forces engaged in a pitched battle on a main thoroughfare.[14] The state-appointed police, or the Mets as they were called, finally won out and assumed full police control of the city, a power wielded by them for thirteen years. State control spread quickly and the plan was adopted by Baltimore in 1860, St. Louis and Chicago in 1861, Kansas City in 1862, Detroit in 1865, and Cleveland in 1866. State control was doomed to fail, however, as it was not uniformly applied within states which adopted enacting legislation. Furthermore, citizens and politicians in cities were not going to stand idly by and pay taxes to support police departments over which they had no control. Some state police boards were maintained for only a year or two, while others persisted for decades.

## THE EFFECT OF THE CIVIL WAR AND RECONSTRUCTION
## ON POLICE OPERATIONS

The Civil War and the period of reconstruction that followed had a devastating impact on many police departments, especially those in the South. The continuity of local government was shattered, police reform was retarded, and stormy politics and social upheaval became the order of the day. In a number of cases, civil policing was suspended and the Army filled the enforcement gap. In those cases where civil authorities retained the authority to police their communities, law enforcement officers were often ousted for political reasons. During the reconstruction of the South, men who had allied themselves with the Confederacy, as most had, were generally disenjoined from participating in government. The result of this bitter experience was to be felt for many years in the South as Southern law enforcement fell far behind law enforcement in other sections of the country. Texas' experience in this regard is somewhat typical.

Texas seceded from the Union in 1861 and joined the Confederacy. While very little war action was conducted on Texas soil, a group called Terry's Texas Rangers, led by Colonel Benjamin

---

[14]George W. Walling, *Recollections of a New York Chief of Police* (New York: 1887), Ch. 4.

Terry and made up of many Texas Rangers and former members, managed to involve itself in innumerable military encounters. During the post-Civil War period, the Texas Rangers were reorganized under the direction of Reconstructionist Governor E.J. Davis and charged with the enforcement of unpopular "carpetbagger" laws. The force quickly fell into disrepute among Texans and it was years before it retained the trust and confidence of the citizenry.

When New Orleans was captured in 1861, civil government was disbanded, martial law was established, and the military, under a provost marshal, took over the duties of policing the city. Following the war, attempts were made to establish a professional police force, but it was 1898 before one was created.

The Southern states were not alone in experiencing problems caused by the Civil War. Northern states, too, experienced difficulties, some of which were created by the Federal provision that permitted draftees to buy their way out of the Union Army by paying three hundred dollars to the government. Laboring men, reasoning correctly that it was a rich man's law, displayed their

Resisting the draft during the Civil War. In 1863 the bloodiest riot in history occurred when mobs protesting President Lincoln's draft call roamed New York City, burning, looting, and lynching. In three days 1,200 were killed and 8,000 were wounded. *(Courtesy of Patterson Smith Publishing Corp.)*

displeasure with the provision by staging a series of draft riots, the most notable of which occurred in New York City in 1863.

## CONCLUSION

The creation of urban American police systems was a necessary and desirable occurrence. Like many other governmental innovations however, it was a concept that was late in coming and one that was fraught with problems. In rapidly industrializing societies there has almost always been a gap between what government accomplished and what was actually needed by citizens. The case of law enforcement was no exception. America was reaching the crossroads of an era, one in which the old ideas and methods of a basically rural country would rapidly change to those of a more dynamic, urban society. Law enforcement was about to enter an era of chaos and confusion, a period of high crime, social crises, and militancy. The police were ill-equipped to handle the challenge, so certain basic innovations would be undertaken to professionalize law enforcement. Yet, even though America's police had come under rather scathing criticism from journalists, public officials, and professors, and stories abounded about their inefficiency and incompetence, there existed a bond between the general community and policemen. Police officers, with all their faults, were still viewed by most citizens as public servants who fulfilled a critical function and who deserved respect because of the very nature of their job. There were, in fact, few community relations problems because the community looked on their police departments as social service agencies. And the police responded by lodging indigents in jail overnight, by providing daily free meals to the needy, who could be seen each night lining up in the rear of precinct houses as patrolmen ladled out soup; by using horse-drawn paddy wagons as ambulances, by delivering Christmas food baskets to the underprivileged, and by providing similar social services. The police, however, were to lose this bond with the community, for as police departments became larger, better equipped, and more professional, they also became isolated and aloof from the citizens they had sworm to serve. Social services performed by early municipal forces were eventually turned over to *ad hoc* agencies so that the police could get on with the business of policing. This problem—to professionalize the police without losing public respect—has been a recurring historical dilemma and one that has persisted to this day.

In 1861 President Abraham Lincoln's life was saved by Allan Pinkerton *(pictured above walking behind Lincoln),* who learned of an assassination plot and warned the President.

*Chapter 5*

# POLICING THE OLD WEST (1848-1890)

The treacherous environment of the Old West created special problems in law enforcement, especially in light of the fact that formal policing was not always available to those who needed it most. In some cases the absence of policemen prompted citizens to band together in groups to protect their lives and property from those who would take advantage of the vulnerability of scattered settlements. All too often, these groups went too far in enforcing the law and maintaining order and the result was a form of collective citizen lawlessness which terrorized the very people they sought to protect. When law enforcement officers were available—generally in raucous cattle towns, mining camps, and port cities—they often were little better than their adversaries. In truth, many sheriffs and marshals had been desperadoes prior to their entry into police ranks. The West was fraught with danger, and the early pioneers—be they homesteaders, cattlemen, miners, or entrepreneurs—had to provide for their safety. They could not concern themselves with the legal niceties that Easterners took for granted. If law enforcement was often harsh and brutal, it was in response to a harsh and brutal environment. The name of the game was survival, and extreme measures were needed to insure that survival. There were four general types of Western law enforcement: extralegal citizen police, formal police, legal citizen police. and parapolice. Some communities had police systems which combined several of the above groupings, while others suspended formal policing during times of crisis so that extralegal but more effective methods could be employed.

## EXTRALEGAL CITIZEN POLICE

From the earliest times, the American West was the home of two contrasting personalities—the honest settler and the outlaw. Both sought a home and a profitable existence, but each pursued it in a decidedly different manner. In the absence of formal law enforcement and criminal justice systems, citizens found it necessary to band together to provide a defense against those who would plunder, steal, and kill. Vigilance committees, groups of organized citizen volunteers which patrolled towns to guard against "evil," sprang up across the West. Although vigilante methods were used in all Western states, they were first employed in California where the lure of gold attracted a human mess which threatened to legitimize murder as a form of social expression. Of all California communities, law and order seemed to have been scarcest in early San Francisco.

From the gold rush days to the dawning of the twentieth century, citizens in San Francisco consistently found it necessary to form vigilance committees. Between 1849 and 1854 it was estimated that California experienced 4,200 murders, almost half of which occurred in San Francisco.[1] In 1851 San Francisco's first vigilance committee was organized "for the protection of the lives and property of the citizens and residents of the city. . . ." A constitution was framed and regular meetings were held to plan strategy. The committee's first official act was to capture, try, and hang, in full view of the citizenry, a suspected burglar, John Jenkins, who earned the dubious honor of being the key figure in the first public execution in America. Three more executions within ninety days convinced the lawless that San Francisco was no longer a safe haven for them, and a measure of order was brought to the city. Several other committees were formed over the years, the most famous being the Committee of Public Safety, formed in 1877, and headed by William T. Coleman, a businessman. The most dramatic achievement of the organization was to muster 3,000 citizens to hang a gambler suspected of killing a county supervisor.[2] However, contrary to popular belief, the vigilance committees were not hysterical lynch mobs bent on violence and revenge. Most were made up of honest men who, because of circumstances not of their own making, were forced to take collective action to protect their communities. The first San

[1] Leroy R. Hafen and Carl Coke Rister, *Western America,* 2nd ed. (Englewood Cliffs, New Jersey: Prentice-Hall, Inc., 1950), pp. 441-442.

[2] N. Ray Gilmore and Gladys Gilmore, *Readings in California History* (New York: Thomas Y. Crowell Company, 1966), pp. 190-191.

Francisco vigilance committee, for example, tried ninety-one cases: forty-one defendants were subsequently released; fifteen were remanded to local law enforcement authorities; fourteen were banished; one was whipped, and only four were hanged.

Vigilance committees were created in Arizona, Montana, Colorado, and Nevada. In fact, every important mining town in the West experimented at one time or another with the idea. Although the name of the organization was different in each community—some were called committees, some were referred to as vigilantes, still others coined the term "regulators"—the function remained the same: root out and punish wrongdoers. As formal policing reached the West vigilance passed out of vogue, except on an *ad hoc* basis.

## FORMAL POLICE

The coming of formal policing to the West was an immensely important phenomenon in the history of American law enforcement. The exploits (sometimes fictionalized) of legendary western lawmen so captured the imagination of the young nation that the extreme methods employed by these officers achieved a degree of legitimacy in the public eye. Although extreme police methods did not originate in the West, romanticized accounts of the police enterprise west of the Mississippi molded public opinion on what the role of a policeman—any policeman—ought to be. Thanks to the image created for lawmen by the Eastern press, the ideal policeman was viewed as one who (1) was large in stature, (2) was harsh in attitude, (3) possessed a low point of tolerance, (4) was courageous in the extreme, and (5) possessed ample firepower and the will to use it. What appeared to be most important to the public was the effectiveness of lawmen in dealing with their adversaries. Apparently there was little concern over the absence of reasonable standards of humane conduct toward criminals or suspected criminals. The swashbuckling methods of Western sheriffs and marshals served as examples for police officers in all sections of the country to emulate. The legacy of the Western lawman—extreme individual action, restricted loyalties, a belief that order must be kept at all costs, a reliance on firearms to settle disputes—can be seen to this day.

## The Texas Rangers[3]

In 1823 Stephen F. Austin hired a body of ten men to protect one of Texas' early settlements from bandits and marauding Indians. The ten were ordered to "range" wide areas of the frontier and guard against unwelcome intruders. On the eve of Texas' War for Independence, the group was enlarged to twenty-five men and officially named the Texas Rangers.

When, in 1845, Texas was admitted to the union, the Rangers became the first official state police agency in America. Their primary job was to protect the state's scattered settlements from Indian incursions while Samuel Houston's ragged army waged its

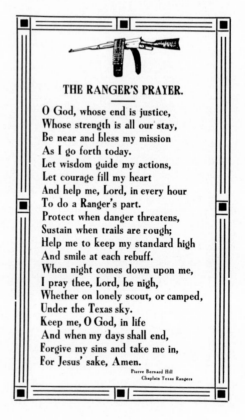

THE RANGER'S PRAYER.
——
O God, whose end is justice,
Whose strength is all our stay,
Be near and bless my mission
As I go forth today.
Let wisdom guide my actions,
Let courage fill my heart
And help me, Lord, in every hour
To do a Ranger's part.
Protect when danger threatens,
Sustain when trails are rough;
Help me to keep my standard high
And smile at each rebuff.
When night comes down upon me,
I pray thee, Lord, be nigh,
Whether on lonely scout, or camped,
Under the Texas sky.
Keep me, O God, in life
And when my days shall end,
Forgive my sins and take me in,
For Jesus' sake, Amen.

Pierre Bernard Hill
Chaplain Texas Rangers

[3]Compiled and excerpted from the following publications obtained from the State of Texas: *The Texas Ranger; The Story of the Texas Rangers; Badges With History; A Brief Sketch of Texas Ranger History;* and from Walter Prescott Webb's book, *The Story of the Texas Rangers.*

war against Santa Anna. The war years saw the Rangers' strength increased to that of a small army, and while they did fight in the Mexican War, their primary duty, the protection of settlements, remained the same. When in 1848 the war with Mexico ended, Rangers' duties were expanded to combat cattle thievery and outlaw activities along the Rio Grande, a task they performed with great gusto and efficiency. Texas Ranger exploits soon became legendary. When the Indian problem abated, the Rangers turned their full attention to capturing, or killing, desperadoes, who were now plaguing the state. Each Ranger captain was furnished with a list containing 3,000 names—thieves, robbers, and highwaymen all. Sometimes the methods of this early police force were questionable: on one occasion the killer of an Army major was hanged without benefit of judge or jury. But the times dictated the methods, and frontier Texas was an untamed land. The following quote by a Ranger captain describes the Rangers' policy for dealing with bandits:

> We're after bandits. If they stampede, pick you out the nearest one to you. Keep him in front of you and keep after him, get as close to him as you can before you shoot. It makes no difference in what direction he goes, stay with him until the finish. These are picked men, and they say they can cope with any Ranger or regulars. If we can overhaul them in the open country, we will teach them a lesson they will never forget.

Tactics notwithstanding, the Rangers brought a measure of law and order to Texas. Famous outlaws such as Sam Bass, King Fisher, and John Wesley Hardin had their careers terminated violently in the Lone Star State. The requirements for becoming a Ranger were simple. Applicants had to be big, tough, and unafraid of physical combat. The stock questions posed to prospective recruits were, Can you shoot? Can you ride? Can you cook? Three consecutive affirmative answers all but assured one of a job.

## Policing the Towns

Town policing also gained a special place in American history. Names such as Wild Bill Hickok, Wyatt Earp, Pat Garrett, and Bat Masterson have achieved a degree of immortality, due in no small measure to the electronic and print media's efforts to chronicle the heroic exploits of Western lawmen, even if truth came off second-best in the telling. The towns in which many early policemen toiled—Dodge City, Tombstone, San Antonio, Laramie,

Cheyenne, El Paso—also gained an unremitting place in history. The law enforcement experience of Wichita, Kansas, a cowtown, was in many ways typical of other Western communities. In 1870 Wichita appointed its first formal lawman, a marshal; he lasted less than one month. Three more marshals were appointed, each leaving after several weeks on the job. It was not unexpected that men were not particularly enthusiastic about risking life and limb for seventy-five dollars a month. In 1871 Michael Meagher was appointed as Wichita city marshal. The following account of Meagher's activities is from the official records of the Wichita Police Department:

> During the early cowtown days of Wichita, the rougher elements of the city were brought under control by Meagher and his small force, supplemented by "special officers" during the cattle drive months. By the time that Wichita's most publicized lawman, Wyatt Earp, was hired as a sixty-dollar-a-month policeman in Meagher's department, the cowtown era was nearing an end in Wichita. It must be assumed from the record that Earp learned a great deal about law enforcement from Mike Meagher, who during his five years in Wichita was able to handle any situation that arose, from disarming a drunken, revolver-shooting cowboy to arresting wild and desperate men. It was from Meagher that Earp learned his technique of applying a long barrel of a six-shooter to the skull of a riotous cowboy.

From this early foundation, the Wichita police system evolved into a competent police agency. In 1897 Wichita established a significant precedent by popularly electing Sam Jones town marshal, the first Negro in history to hold that post.

### LEGAL CITIZEN POLICE

Western communities that commissioned formal law enforcement officers often found it necessary to assist and support them in very practical ways. When a situation arose that could not be handled by the police, citizens were called in to supplement the force, which, more often than not, consisted of one man—a sheriff or a marshal. These "casual deputies," as they were called, acted as an enthusiastic police reserve to be pressed into duty as posses, jail guards, and replacements when the town police were away.

The ancient concepts of hue and cry and watch and ward were used in Western communities, whose citizenry viewed pragmatically the need for mutual protection and assistance. An almost family-like cooperation existed between law enforcement and the community, and Western sheriffs often resembled the tithingmen of old. Citizen involvement with the police, as much as any other factor, eventually fused the scattered early settlements and mining camps into homogeneous communities.

## PARAPOLICE

Most Western towns did not have strong, effective police forces, and even those few that did could not provide all the needed public safety services. The great open spaces between towns had virtually no police protection, a factor that took on new significance with the advent of stagecoaches and the railroads. As prosperity hit the West, companies were forced to transport large quantities of gold, silver, and cash across desolate areas, many of which were infested by badmen. In order to protect their interests, mining companies, stagecoach lines, banks, railroads, shipping concerns, and merchant associations hired private guards to safeguard valuable cargo. These early parapolice officers were at first assigned to "ride shotgun" on cash and bullion shipments. However, as crime rates soared, the responsibilities of parapolicemen were expanded. Although most officers were employed directly by the companies they policed, private detective agencies were formed by men who viewed Western lawlessness, or at least the policing of it, as an exiting and lucrative way of making a living. These agencies hired themselves out to the highest bidder and, in so doing, changed the philosophy of private policing from prevention to detection and apprehension. Many of the more dynamic private police forces not only performed guard service but tracked down and arrested dangerous criminals. Of the scores of private detective agencies, none was more famous or more effective than the legendary Pinkertons.

## The Pinkerton Detective Agency

The Pinkerton Detective Agency was founded by Allan Pinkerton in Chicago in 1850. Although much of its later activities were directed at the breaking of strikes in the East, a major part of its early functions included tracking down Western desperadoes, especially train robbers, a task it fulfilled rather effectively. Allan Pinkerton, who had been the City of Chicago's first detective, was a gifted man whose exploits were nationally known. He organized the secret service division of the United States Army in 1861 and was made its first chief. Later, while employed by the Wilmington and Baltimore Railroad, he saved Abraham Lincoln's life by uncovering an assassination plot directed against the President.[4] In the West, fragmented police agencies—most of which consisted of one man who was overworked and underpaid—were often powerless to act against the badmen of the day, and the Pinkertons were hired by mining companies and railroads to fill the law enforcement void. More than one train robber who had alluded a sheriff and his *ad hoc* deputies ended up in a fatal confrontation with a well-armed force of Pinkerton men. Pinkertons labored under few of the constraints that limited formal law officers: they recognized no jurisdictional boundaries; politics were of little regard to them; legal restraints were often ignored. Consequently, they enjoyed a string of successes of which few police agencies of the time—public or private—could boast. But even though the Pinkerton Detective Agency performed a valuable and necessary function, it often did so with an enthusiasm that ignored the rules of law. For example, in a raid on the suspected hideout of the notorious Jesse James, a thirty-two-pound iron bomb, wrapped in flaming, kerosene-saturated rags, was thrown into the suspected hideaway. After the explosion it was discovered that Jesse had fled earlier, but his mother and his small brother had not. The young boy was killed and his mother lost her right arm. Public opinion polarized against the Pinkertons over the incident and Jesse James was on his way to becoming a folk hero, thanks in no small measure to the ill-advised action of the famous detective agency.[5] Yet, in the Pinkertons' defense it must be said that many of their own men had fallen in battles with outlaws; some had been shot in ambush. The bitterness of the post-Civil War period led to violent and bloody clashes between Eastern detectives and Western badmen, who robbed and murdered in the name of a defeated cause (The Confederacy) and who looked on themselves as guerrillas rather than outlaws. The Pinkertons employed methods of questionable morality, but they did a job which, in its way, helped bring a semblance of order to the West.

[4]Paul B. Weston and Kenneth M. Wells, *Criminal Investigation* (Englewood Cliffs, New Jersey: Prentice-Hall, Inc., 1970), pp. 9-11.

[5]Carl W. Breihan, *Jesse James* (New York: Frederick Fell, Inc., 1953), pp. 118-120.

## CONCLUSION

The early Western lawmen—be they citizens, policemen, or parapolicemen—have gained a place in this country's history.

A motley crew of misdemeanants en route to the local lockup. *(Courtesy of the Kansas City Police Department)*

Authors have portrayed these pioneers as either heroes or villains. They were, in fact, average men who were pressed into service to fight a battle against crime and violence. Some used excessive force in fulfilling their responsibilities and many were drawn toward law enforcement careers for all the wrong reasons. But in the main, Western citizens received better police protection than they paid for and infinitely better protection than they deserved. For less than one-hundred dollars a month sheriffs and marshals risked their lives nightly. Casual deputies, virtually unpaid, often pursued and arrested professional killers. Parapolicemen with no special training hunted down some of the most notorious desperadoes in the West. The price of policing the West was high, however, as untold numbers of officers forfeited their lives in defense of their communities.

August Vollmer, Chief of Police, Berkeley, California (1905-1932). This picture was taken about the time of his retirement June 30, 1932. Most of the time, after becoming Chief, Vollmer wore a business suit, but on special occasions, such as reviewing his officers, he did wear a uniform. *(Courtesy of Alfred E. Parker, Catalina Island, California)*

*Chapter 6*

# LAW ENFORCEMENT IN THE GILDED AGE (1866-1919)

$T$ he late nineteenth century seemed to be characterized by corruption, materialism, and an indifference to many old American ideas and values. Mark Twain was so disenchanted with the era that he sardonically termed it "the Gilded Age," a name that has struck.[1] The simple and genial philosophies that the country had known for years—romantic, optimistic, heavily religious, individualistic in nature—were to be subjected to the new order, a social, economic, and industrial revolution. Whether the changes that this revolution created were desirable is a question best left for others to answer. America, for good or ill, was changing and it presented an enormous problem for law enforcement officials.

Between 1860 and 1910, America's urban population increased sevenfold. Cities with more than 50,000 inhabitants increased from 16 to 109. The population of New York City jumped from one million to over three million. As might be expected, crime rose astronomically over this period. American society was becoming more dynamic, more complex, increasingly impersonal, and of utmost importance, more mobile; yet the police had no state extradition laws, no criminal records or crime statistics, and no system of interdepartmental communications. Fragmented police departments were still using rural methods to police an increasingly urban society. Realizing that they were fighting a losing battle against crime and violence, some forward-thinking police executives decided to band together in a professional association that would work to solve their problems.

---

[1]Richard N. Current, T. Harry Williams, and Frank Freidel, *American History: A Survey* (New York: Alfred A. Knopf, Inc., 1964), p. 561.

## A NATIONAL POLICE CHIEFS' ASSOCIATION[2]

Early in 1871 St. Louis Police Chief James McDonough proposed that "a convention of the heads of police forces of every city in the union be held to inaugurate and adopt a code of rules and regulations whereby the whole detective force of the country can act in unison for the prevention and detection of crime." Later that year, 112 police officials met in convention to discuss the increase in crime, the apparent breakdown in the morals of young people, alcoholism, and other related topics, including the subject of a uniform crime-reporting system. No clear-cut decisions were made at the meeting, although one thing became clear: a permanent association of police chiefs was needed. However, it was not until twenty-two years later that real progress was made in that direction. In 1893 Chief William S. Seavey of Omaha proposed a meeting of police executives in Chicago. Fifty-one chiefs of police attended to discuss "matters of mutual interest." The primary topic was the desirability of mutual cooperation to suppress crime and apprehend criminals. The five-day meeting was so successful that it was decided that a permanent organization should be immediately formed. Objectives were defined, a constitution was drafted, and the National Chiefs of Police Union was born. In 1902 the group decided to change its name to the International Association of Chiefs of Police (IACP), a name which it still bears. The first major contribution of the IACP was the establishment of a central clearing house for criminal identification records. The clearing house was later converted to a fingerprint repository. Cities desiring to make use of the repository were assessed between ten and one hundred dollars per annum, depending on their size. Over the years, the IACP was to evolve into one of the most innovative institutions in law enforcement and one that worked, often against tremendous odds, to professionalize the American police service. Later chapters chronicle the IACP's total contribution to policing.

### THE SEARCH FOR AN IDEAL SYSTEM OF POLICE ADMINISTRATION

#### The Decline of State Control

Toward the end of the nineteenth century, the system of state

[2]Excerpted from "IACP," *The Police Chief,* September 1969, pp. 37-39.

control of municipal police departments began to decline, partly because of its lack of success—it did not end corruption, it simply changed the corruptors—and partly because local political bosses could not ply their evil trade without controlling police operations, so they went about restoring the needed control. The decline of state control over police forces actually began in 1868 when the Democratic party, at a convention in Cleveland, sounded the cry for home rule, a not unexpected maneuver considering that Democratic machinery ran most urban areas. The precedent for ending state domination was established in New York City by one of America's classic figures of corruption, Boss Tweed.

William Marcy Tweed, mayor of New York City, was a man who thought big. Tweed's Ring, as his political machine was called, set out to rob the city of some 200 million dollars. The state-controlled police force was a hindrance to Boss Tweed, so he swept it aside and set out to fulfill his master plan of graft and corruption. So extensive became his largesse that almost the entire system of criminal justice was purported to be either on his payroll or afraid to defy him.[3] Said the *New York Times.*[4]

> Our independent police department, which has given us a disciplined and uniformed force in place of a vagabond band of ragamuffins, will yield obedience to that power which demands free rum and votes and gives us police justices who set free fully one-half of all the villains the police properly arrest.

By analyzing Tweed's massive financial empire, the *New York Times* was able to present front page evidence of millions of dollars in graft, thus forcing city policemen into action. One by one Tweed's Ring was arrested until the Boss himself was tried and convicted. Tweed went to jail, where he stayed until his death. The end of state control was a desirable occurrence; but all too often the system that replaced it was one of corrupt political domination, as in New York City. Boss Tweed in many ways typified the cross that honest urban policemen and administrators were forced to bear in the Gilded Age. Three more systems of police administration were to be tried before a workable principle was found: the bipartisan board, the commission government plan, and unified administrative leadership.

[3]John Lofton, *Justice and the Press* (Boston: Beacon Press, 1966), pp. 78-79.

[4]Raymond B. Fosdick, *American Police Systems* (New York: The Century Co., 1920), pp. 94-95.

## Birth and Death of the Bipartisan
## Administrative Board

The idea behind the bipartisan administrative board, which was in vogue for a short time toward the end of the century, was that politics could never be eliminated from the management of police departments. So a board made up of representatives of both political parties offered the most impartial administrative system. The reasoning was that one partisan administrator could watch another, thus eliminating corrupting influences. The bipartisan principle proved to be unsuccessful in its aim to lessen the influence of politics by taking the police department out of the hands of a single party; in actuality, political influence was simply compounded by turning it over to both parties, which often formed an unholy alliance to thwart aggressive law enforcement. The largest city to try the short-lived concept was Philadelphia.

## Enter and Exit the Commission-Government Plan

The next major innovation in police administration came at the turn of the century with the creation of commission government in a number of cities. The concept embodied the integration of legislative and executive powers in a small commission elected at large by popular vote. One member of the commission was designated to be commissioner of public safety, his authority encompassing police and fire operations, the enforcement of building codes, and health and welfare services. The International City Managers' Association termed the concept "amateur supervision by a popularly-elected, transient police administrator. . . complicated by the demands of other important municipal services.[5] Although some communities still use the plan, it fell into disrepute early in the game and many cities which adopted it turned to other methods.

## Single Executive Control

After years of trial and error a system of single executive control emerged as the most reasonable and efficient method of operating a police agency. In this system, one man—in theory a professional—was directly appointed by a city's ruling body (or

[5]International City Managers' Association, *Municipal Police Administration,* fifth edition (Washington: International City Managers' Association, 1961), p. 44.

elected by the community) to run the police department. Unified administrative leadership, even today the best proven method of administering police operations, dramatically pointed up the folly of multiple control.

## The Search for a Method

In groping for a workable method of administering police operations, major cities went through truly agonizing searches for an "ideal system." Experiment after experiment was tried, but most proved unworkable. Each time a scandal occurred in a police department, public outrage dictated a change in the police organizational setup. The experience in Cincinnati illustrates the unhappy wanderings of a city in search of a method:[6]

1859—Board of four commissioners appointed by mayor, police judge, and city auditor.

1860—Board abolished; Chief of police appointed by the mayor.

1873—Board of four commissioners popularly elected.

1874—Control by mayor reestablished.

1877—Board of of five commissioners appointed by governor.

1880—Control of mayor reestablished.

1885—Board of three commissioners appointed by local board of public works.

1886—Board of four commissioners appointed by governor.

1902—Board of four commissioners appointed by mayor and council. . . .

By way of summary, six major methods of controlling police operations were attempted by municipal and state governments in the nineteenth and early twentieth centuries:

1. Popular elections.
2. Partisan administrative Boards.
3. State control.
4. Bipartisan administrative boards.
5. Commission-government plans.
6. Single executive control.

All, save the last method, proved in varying ways unsuccessful.

## THE CORRUPTION ISSUE

Police corruption in the post-Civil War era was conspicuous. It

[6]*Supra* note 4, p. 112.

was a time of big city political bosses, and policemen often had to either cooperate with grafting politicians, ignore obvious violations of the law, or seek other employment. Much police corruption was of the minor variety. The story of a Boston police detective, George S. Chapman, was typical. Chapman, on an assignment to watch for a congregation of pickpockets in Hartford in 1867, was himself arrested for pickpocketing.[7] However, in a disturbing number of cases it was the system of law enforcement and government that was corrupt, and officers were simply swept up in a tide which they could neither control nor resist.

## The San Francisco "System"[8]

In many ways the story of San Francisco at the turn of the century was illustrative of the malaise that gripped a number of the country's major cities. Corruption pervaded every component of local government, including, of course, the police department. It was the type of corruption that began at the top of the governmental structure—with the mayor, the board of supervisors, and the police commission—and spread down the pyramid until even the beat patrolmen were effected by it. Under the San Francisco "system" certain favored individuals were given immunity to the law in return for a fee, usually a substantial one, to the right person—the mayor's "representative." Gamblers were allowed to ply their trade, and certain other classes of vice flourished openly. As a result, a virtual reign of terror prevailed. Street robberies were a daily occurrence. Merchants were robbed in broad daylight. Honest citizens were afraid to walk the streets at night. Although street crimes were prevalent, the most substantial criminal income was made in city hall. For example, the mayor decided that it was a good idea to extract large sums of money from the city's "French Restaurants." In San Francisco, the term "French Restaurant" meant any establishment which contained a public restaurant on the ground floor and private supper bedrooms on the second floor. Not unexpectedly these places did a good deal of

[7]Roger Lane, *Policing the City—Boston 1822-1885* (Cambridge: Harvard University Press, 1967), p. 146.

[8]A full account of the San Francisco "system" may be found in Franklin Hichborn's *The System* (Montclair, New Jersey: Patterson Smith Publishing Corp. Originally published in 1915; reprinted in 1969.)

business. The mayor, in collusion with the police commission and the police chief, revoked the liquor license of a French Restaurant known as Tortoni's. All other French Restaurants in the city were notified that when their licenses expired they would not be renewed because of trumped up violations of the city code. The police commission had arbitrary power to revoke licenses. Without a liquor license, which had to be renewed every three months, the restaurants could not remain in business. One of the police commissioners would not agree to the mayor's plan, so he was summarily dismissed and replaced by a more cooperative commissioner. As everything appeared darkest to the French Restaurant Association, an attorney magically appeared on the scene guaranteeing the proprietors that he, for a fee, could get their licenses renewed. The Association signed a contract with the attorney—the mayor's man—for a fat fee and they were never again bothered.

Just as crime and violence threatened to revive San Francisco's committees of vigilance, the district attorney, an honest public official, assisted by a small group of policemen, initiated a probe which ended with the arrest and indictment of the mayor and the chief of police, the resignation of sixteen San Francisco supervisors, and the shocking exposé of the "system" to the rest of the state and the nation. The later trials, known as The San Francisco Graft Prosecution, were marred by extreme violence. On one occasion a witness' home was dynamited. On another an assistant district attorney was shot down as he stood in his courtroom. However, in the end, the corruptors were imprisoned for their crimes and a virtual revolution in city government ended the San Francisco "system."

## THE PENDLETON ACT: AN END TO THE SPOILS ERA

Police corruption in the Gilded Age was a complex phenomenon. To allege that it was caused by one or two social, economic, or political factors is to perpetrate an inaccuracy, for it was a multifaceted problem. The police were badly trained, poorly equipped, overworked, underpaid, and politically dominated, to mention but a few of the early wrongs. In simplest terms the environment of the era made it exceedingly difficult to be an honest policeman. In 1883 the Federal Government, reacting to the assassination of President James Garfield by a frustrated office-seeker, passed the Pendleton Act, thus ending seventy-five years of the "spoils system," at least at some governmental levels.

The Pendleton Act of 1883 was a civil service law which "classified" a limited number of Federal jobs so that applicants would have to be chosen by competitive written examinations. To administer the Act, a bipartisan civil service commission was established. Initially only 14,000 of 100,000 positions were placed on the classified list, but within a half-century a majority of Federal employees were under civil service.

Although the Pendleton Act did not apply to municipal government, it did set a precedent for civil service coverage. The Federal Government's success with the system motivated many communities to adopt it. The enactment of civil service regulations in many cities eliminated one causative element of police corruption, but only one.

### THE ADVANCE OF TECHNOLOGY: A TWO-EDGED SWORD

The years following the Civil War saw a flood of inventions and technological innovations. In the entire history of the United States to 1860 only 36,000 patents had been issued, but from 1860 to 1890 there were 440,000! Police departments did not rush to take advantage of technological achievements, although a few law enforcement agencies did employ some of the new-fangled devices. In 1867 the first call boxes were installed for use by patrolmen in selected urban areas. By 1878 police in the District of Columbia had installed telephones in precincts, the first police agency in the country to use the device on a regular basis. In 1880 the Chicago Police Department was first to use a combined telephone and telegraph call box system. Chicago in 1884 established the country's first criminal identification bureau. The New York Police Department, emulating the private shipping industry, in 1908 became the first police department to install wireless telegraph on its patrol boats. Probably the most grisly use of technology occurred in 1891 when New York became the first state to electrocute a man for murder.

The advent of technology also had a negative impact on law enforcement, partly because of social pressures—society became increasingly impersonal, dynamic, and complex—and partly

During the late 1800s a novel communication system was developed in Chicago by the Gamewell Telephone and Telegraph System. Boxes equipped with telephones were installed at various places throughout a city so that patrolmen and citizens could immediately communicate with police head-quarters. This, the Gamewell System, was the forerunner of today's modern call boxes. *(Courtesy of the New Haven Police Department)*

because criminals often seemed to make better use of the new achievements than did the police. Burglars replaced gunpowder with nitroglycerin. Safes were entered and locks picked with burglarly devices of enormous complexity. The development of systems of transportation made it easy for criminals of all types to achieve a degree of mobility previously denied them. The police, on the other hand, were virtually trapped within arbitrarily set political boundaries—city limits, county lines, state lines.

The old and the new of another era. On the left, a Bertillion operator measures a suspect's body for identification purposes; while on the right, a fingerprint technician illustrates the identification method that replaced the Bertillion system. *(Courtesy of the Chicago Police Department)*

The science of criminal investigation began to emerge in the post-Civil War period, spurred on by the advance of technology and the growing sophistication of criminals. The new science was truly an international phenomenon as scientists from scores of countries invented new concepts and improved existing ones. In 1883 Alphonse Bertillion, a youthful employee in the identification division of the Prefecture of Police in Paris, conducted a survey of his files which indicated that no two people had the

same physical measurements. As a result of the survey, Bertillion developed the first system of criminal identification. Responding to criticism from Paris policemen that they could not stop and measure each suspect they encountered, Bertillion created a system of visual identification which concentrated on the characteristics of a person's head. The size and shape of a man's head was categorized along with descriptions of certain facial features until a portrait of him emerged. Positive identification of a suspect could then be made from photographs. This system was called portrait parlé. In 1892 a method called fingerprints began to replace portrait parlé as a system of personal identification. The concept was not new; the Chinese had experimented with it over one thousand years before. However, an English scientist named Francis Galton offered conclusive proof of the uniqueness of individual fingerprints. The discovery that no two fingerprints were alike furnished police agencies with a criminal identification method of revolutionary proportions. Nine years later Sir Richard Henry developed a system for classifying fingerprints which allowed clerks to have speedy access to print files. In 1910 an American, Albert Gross, developed a system of authenticating questioned documents and for the first time American courts accepted as admissable scientific evidence in this area.

## LABOR MILITANCY AND THE POLICE

The Gilded Age saw the rise of "big business." As business became big, consolidated, and national in its scope, it was inevitable that labor would attempt to follow suit and create an organization that would match the power of capital. Laboring men, not unexpectedly, wanted a bigger piece of the action. Thwarting their efforts, however, were unresponsive management and a hostile, antiunion public. During the early years of trade unionism, disputes between labor and management consistently deteriorated into extreme collective violence. All too often poorly trained, ill-equipped, and outnumbered police departments found themselves thrust into these controversies. In a number of cases labor violence was confronted and suppressed by management without police help, there being no formal law enforcement in some turbulent areas. A few of the more dramatic manifestations involved extremist groups like the Molly Maguires (1870s); but most violent and bloody occurrences simply involved the police or para-policemen and angry working men. Typical were the Haymarket Affair (1886), the Carnegie Steel Strike (1892), and the Great Strikes of 1917-1919.

## The Molly Maguires[9]

The Molly Maguires was a secret society whose members ter-

[9]Walter J. Coleman, *Labor Disturbances in Pennsylvania, 1850-1880* (New York: Arno Press, 1936, reprinted 1970).

rorized the eastern Pennsylvania coal fields in the early 1870s. The Mollies were of the ancient order of the Hibernians, a group that had revolted against their landlords in Ireland and who now rebelled against English mine owners in America. The Molly Maguires intimidated coal operators with such direct methods as murder. There being no effective formal police forces in the eastern Pennslyvania region at the time, the Philadelphia and Reading Railroad—owner of most of the mines—set out to engage parapolice help. The indomitable Pinkertons were contacted and they agreed to send one of their most capable investigators, Detective James McParlan, to infiltrate the Mollies. McParlan worked his way into the organization and became a Molly leader. As a result of his undercover exploits, authorities were able to arrest, convict, and execute many Mollies, thereby curtailing their reign of tyranny.

On May 4, 1886, an anarchist threw a bomb into a formation of Chicago policemen in Haymarket Square. Eight officers were killed and sixty-seven others were wounded in one of the blackest moments in police history. *(Courtesy of the Chicago Police Department)*

## The Haymarket Affair[10]

On May 4, 1886, in the midst of a strike at the McCormick Harvester Company in Chicago, a group of anarchists—European radicals who wanted to destroy "class government" by terroristic tactics—called a meeting in Haymarket Square to protest "police harassment" of strikers. During the meeting the Chicago police appeared and ordered the protestors to disperse. Suddenly a bomb was thrown into the phalanx of policemen by an unknown assailant. When the smoke had cleared, eight policemen has been killed and sixty-seven others had been wounded. Chicago officials rounded up eight anarchists and charged them with the murders of the officers on the grounds that they had incited the individual who had thrown the bomb (he was never captured). In a trial heavy with emotion and vituperation, all were convicted and four were condemned to death. The Haymarket Affair polarized public opinion against labor, which was widely thought to be dominated by anarchists and radicals, and it set the tone for future police-labor confrontations.

## The Carnegie Steel Strike[11]

When in 1892 the management of Pennsylvania's Carnegie Steel Company announced that a small group of workers would have to take cuts in salary, trouble followed. Workers shut down the plant and gathered to protest management's action. Management promptly hired three hundred Pinkerton guards to reopen the plant. The Pinkerton Detective Agency was now more a strike-breaking firm than an investigating body. The Pinkertons marched on the plant where they were met by strikers armed with guns, dynamite, clubs, and knives. In the battle that ensued, three guards and ten strikers were killed and hundreds of participants were injured. At the battle's end the Pinkertons surrendered and were unceremoniously escorted from the scene. Management and local police officials petitioned the state for assistance, whereupon some eight thousand National Guard troops were sent to preserve order. They did, but not before an anarchist tried, unsuccessfully, to assassinate a Carnegie executive.

[10]*Supra* note 1, pp. 509-510.

[11]*Ibid.*, p. 511.

## The Great Strikes of 1917-1919

Labor militancy reached its peak in the 1917-1919 period when a wave of strikes spread across the country involving at one time or another more than five million workers, ranging from longshoremen to Metropolitan Opera stars. Time after time, policemen and parapolice firms—notably the Pinkerton Agency—were called upon to man the barricades against strikers. Time and time again blood was spilled by the police and by their adversaries. In many instances troops had to be called out as militant activity went beyond the bounds of reason. However, the police were by no means immune to labor militancy within their own ranks. In 1919 no less than thirty-three police departments had been granted charters from the American Federation of Labor (AFL). By far the most famous case of police-labor militancy occurred in Boston in 1919.

## The Boston Police Strike

In 1919 the lot of Boston's policemen was indeed unhappy. In fact, the conditions under which patrolmen labored were scandalous. Policemen were entitled to but one full day off every fifteen days, and even then were required to obtain written permission from superiors to go beyond the city limits of Boston. Officers, depending on their assignments, worked between seventy-three and ninety-eight hours weekly. The little off-duty time they received was often spent on standby duty in the back rooms of precinct stations. Precincts were old and vermin-ridden and the rickety bunk beds provided for standby officers had to be shared by two men. Although promotional examinations were given by the department, it was perfectly legal for police administrators to ignore top scorers and promote political cronies. In addition to their regular duties, officers were made to fulfill "miscellaneous services" such as delivering unpaid tax bills. For this, patrolmen were paid $1,300 per annum—about twenty-five cents an hour, half of what war-workers made, and considerably less than streetcar motormen earned.[12] In August, 1919, the Boston Social Club, the patrolmen's fraternal organization, petitioned the American Federation of Labor for a union charter, which was granted. Police Commissioner Edwin U. Curtis, out-

[12]*The Boston Globe,* September 9, 1919, p. 12.

The Boston Police Strike of 1919 stunned the nation and brought a quick response from government. On the left is former Superintendent of Police William Pierce, who mobilized a volunteer police force to replace striking officers. On the right, Boston Police Station Number 1 stands vacant in the wake of the strike.

raged at the action, issued an order forbidding union membership; however, the officers, led by the president of their union, Patrolman John F. McInnes, defied the order and refused to disband. Curtis brought McInnes and eighteen other leaders up on departmental charges, tried and convicted them but delayed sentencing in deference to Mayor Andrew J. Peters, who had appointed a committee of thirty-four citizens to try and seek a solution to the problem. The Committee of Thirty-four, as it was called, was headed by James J. Storrow, a dedicated civic leader. The committee came up with a solution to which all the parties, except

Curtis, agreed. The main issue in the settlement involved leniency for the nineteen officers: the patrolmen demanded it; the mayor urged it; and Storrow and his committee recommended it. Where-upon Commissioner Curtis suspended the nineteen. On September 9, 1,117 of Boston's 1,544 policemen went on strike to protest the suspensions.[13] It should be noted that the political atmo-sphere at the time was not conducive to the settling of disputes. The mayor was a Democrat; the Commissioner, a former mayor, was Republican. They had both attended school in New England at competitive institutions. Compounding the problem was the fact that the power to appoint the police commissioner rested not with the mayor but with Governor Calvin Coolidge, a lifelong Republican. Commissioner Curtis failed to mobilize a replacement force for the strikers on the first night of the walkout, leaving the city virtually unprotected. Some historians feel that Curtis' initial

[13]Claud M. Foess, *Calvin Coolidge* (Boston: Little, Brown and Co., 1940), pp. 203-218.

inaction was due to his refusal to believe his men would strike, while others allege that the Commissioner did so to polarize public opinion against the patrolmen. Crime and violence—mostly minor—erupted and troops were dispatched to Boston. A volunteer police force was also organized. Extreme physical force was used by the troops in restoring order: groups of people were indiscriminately fired into; machine guns were turned on a crowd which refused to disperse; gamblers fleeing crap games were fired upon, and on at least one occasion soldiers on horseback with drawn sabers swept Scollay Square clean of people by employing a classic cavalry charge. Throughout the critical stages of the strike, the Governor refused to act or even comment on the affair. Only after civil and military authorities appeared to have the situation under control and public opinion had clearly been mobilized against striking officers did Governor Coolidge release a statement. Stated Coolidge: "There is no right to strike against the public safety by anybody, any time, anywhere!"[14] When the smoke had cleared, the 1,117 strikers were fired, a new police force was hired, and Coolidge, who had become a national hero because of his belated remark, was on the road to the Presidency, an office he was ill-equipped to assume. Boston's action in firing the striking patrolmen set a precedent for dealing with rebellious policemen which lasted for nearly a half-century.[15]

## The Organization of Police Rank and File

Although the general phenomenon of labor militancy had an impact on the internal workings of police departments, the Boston Police Strike was an extreme example of that impact. Few police departments of the day even threatened to strike, much less engage in it. But the country's working men were unionizing and it was only natural that policemen, most of whom came from laboring backgrounds, would organize too. Some affiliated with unions but most banded together in fraternal groups, social clubs, and benevolent associations. While these organizations performed a social role, they also provided the collective strength officers

[14]*Ibid.*, pp. 219-233.

[15]Elmer D. Graper, *American Police Administration* (New York: The Macmillian Co., 1921), p. 318.

needed to press economic issues. They were not unions, but many fulfilled a number of union-like functions. New York City led in the establishment of police rank-and-file organizations with the founding of the Patrolmen's Benevolent Association (PBA) in 1894. Many police forces followed suit and soon these types of groups abounded. Probably the most significant occurrence in this

An early paddy wagon ready for patrol duty—except for buttoning up that blouse! *(Courtesy of the Chicago Police Department)*

area came in 1915, when two Pittsburgh patrolmen, Martin L. Toole and Delbert H Nagle, founded the Fraternal Order of Police (FOP). The FOP soon became a national organization, the primary strength of which centered in the industrial cities of the Northeast. What the labor union was to the worker, the FOP and like organizations became to the policeman. However, the FOP was different from a union in two major respects: (1) it prohibited striking and (2) it enrolled everyone from patrolman to chief. Fifty years after its inception, the FOP was to become one of the largest and most powerful organizations of its type in America.

## THE STATE POLICE

The changing American social scene, now unalterably modified by technology and the predictable events caused by a nation in transition, forced state governments to seek new ways in which to meet the challenges of the era. In 1893 Charles and Frank Duryea built and operated the first gasoline-powered automobile in the United States. Less than twenty-five years later there were nearly five million automobiles on the roads.[16] That, coupled with the inadequacy of the state militia, rural police agencies, and para-police organizations to cope with labor disorders, led state legislatures to consider creating state police agencies.

A number of early state police experiments had been undertaken by some states. In 1835 the Texas Rangers were formed; in 1865 Massachusetts appointed a handful of state constables to suppress commercialized vice, the country's first general state police force; in 1901 the Arizona Rangers were established; while in 1903 Connecticut formed a small state patrol force. In 1905 New Mexico created a mounted patrol to police its borders.[17] But these were small agencies with sharply limited functions and by 1905 it was obvious that a new approach was needed. In that year Pennsylvania, in a sharp break with tradition, created a State Constabulary.

The Pennsylvania State Police Department was as unique from other police forces as night was from day. Other law enforcement agencies had evolved through centuries of painfully gradual development. But, as one police scholar put it, the Pennsylvania force "was not evolved. . .it was made."[18] Traditional concepts of police organization and administration were totally ignored. Recognized and accepted police practices were shunned. The Pennsylvania State Police Force was a revolutionary concept and one that signaled the beginning of a new era in law enforcement administration.

The Pennsylvania State Constabulary was commanded by a superintendent of police, who was responsible only to the governor, an important administrative breakthrough. From its inception, it operated as a mounted and uniformed force assigned to patrol the entire state, not just selected areas. It did this by systematically creating troop headquarters and substations in even the most remote areas of the state. Pennsylvania had created a true

[16]*Supra* note 1, p. 589.

[17]Bruce Smith, *The State Police* (New York: The Macmillian Co., 1925), pp. 34-39.

[18]*Ibid.*, p. 39.

Members of the Pennsylvania State Police in 1906, a year after their founding. President Theodore Roosevelt *(pictured above)* was an enthusiastic backer of the force from the beginning, and he once stated, "I feel so strongly about them that the mere fact that a man is honorably discharged from this Force would make me at once, and without hesitation, employ him for any purpose needing courage, prowess, good judgment, loyalty, and entire trustworthiness." *(Courtesy of the Pennsylvania State Police)*

state police organization. "Both in its scheme of organization, and in its policy of continuous patrol, this organization represented a distinct departure from earlier state practice."[19]

For the next dozen years there was little extension of the state police concept. No new state police forces were formed and existing forces seemed content to expand gradually and adopt the procedures of other state organizations that seemed to be working. In many cases Pennsylvania's Constabulary served as a model. However, in response to emerging traffic problems, labor disorders, and civil turmoil, other states eventually followed the lead of the pioneers.

In 1917 civil unrest prompted New York to establish a state police, modeled after Pennsylvania's idea. That same year, the Colorado Rangers were established. The Michigan State Police was organized in 1917. West Virginia set up a Department of Public Safety. In 1919 New Jersey, Maryland, and Delaware followed

[19]*Ibid.,*p. 40.

suit.[20] By 1920 two distinct types of state forces had evolved: (1) those which had general law enforcement duties and (2) those whose primary responsibility was motor vehicle control. The fledgling state police movement was to meet great resistance from many quarters. Three of the early forces—those in Colorado, Arizona, and New Mexico—were disbanded because of politics. Laboring men often despised the state police, which they believed was established to break strikes. The American Civil Liberties Union was to later initiate court suits to test the legality and constitutionality of many forces. But state police forces survived this early controversy and, in time, received popular public acceptance as a necessary and desirable institution.

## THE RISE OF FEDERAL ENFORCEMENT AGENCIES

Federal law enforcement agencies were created in a rather haphazard fashion by a United States Congress responding to the emergence of selected problems. Most were set up on an *ad hoc* basis, that is their jurisdiction was generally limited to specific crimes or classes of crimes. It was well into the twentieth century before any type of coordinated effort was undertaken to unify fragmented Federal police agencies. Some of the early developments in this area represented a response to crises, rather than the thoughtful and studied implementation of a needed investigative component.

In 1861 Congress appropriated money to "investigate crimes against the United States"; seven years later the Internal Revenue Service appointed twenty-five "detectives." Although Congress passed a bill in 1842 to combat counterfeiting, it was 1865 before the Secret Service was assigned to investigate violations of it. Expanded duties of the Service were to include protection of the President and Vice-President and their immediate families. On June 22, 1870, the United States Attorney General appointed a handful of detectives to investigate the importation of women from Europe for immoral purposes. In 1886 the United States Customs Service organized the Border Patrol. By the first decade of the twentieth century, it became apparent that the Federal Government needed a professional staff of full-time general

---

[20]*Ibid.*, pp. 41-45.

investigators to handle the rising volume of lawlessness, mostly of the white-collar variety, against the Government. Accordingly, in 1908 President Theodore Roosevelt organized the Bureau of Investigation to serve as the investigative branch of the Department of Justice. The Bureau, forerunner of the FBI, was small in number and not noted for its brilliance, at least in the early days.

## THE ADVENT OF WOMEN POLICE

The dawning of the twentieth century saw a good deal of police reform, much of it well accepted by a public tired of inefficient policing, corruption, and a spiraling crime rate. However, some of the early innovations were, to say the least, controversial. One of the most radical new ideas involved the employment of women as police officers.

Although women had been employed as police matrons since 1845, the first actual appointment of a woman to perform police duties came in 1893, when Mrs. Marie Owens, a policeman's widow, was hired by the Chicago Police Department as a "patrolman," a position she held for thirty years.[21] In 1905 Mrs. Lola Baldwin was officially appointed to do "protective work" with young girls at Oregon's Lewis and Clark Centennial Exposition.[22] In 1910 the Los Angeles Police Department appointed the first full-time paid "policewoman" when it hired Mrs. Alice Stebbins Wells. Mrs. Wells was a rather imaginative woman. Prior to her appointment she had conducted a crime survey that concluded, not coincidentally, that there was a crying need for women in police work. Armed with this information, she persuaded a hundred prominent citizens to sign a petition to the mayor demanding that he add her to the police force. Mrs. Wells kept the petition secret so that the antifeminist press would not editorially condemn her and her concept. The mayor, a practical man who interpreted the petition as a mandate from a substantial number of civic leaders, hired Mrs. Wells.

[21] Chloe Owings, *Women Police* (Montclair, New Jersey: Patterson Smith Publishing Corp. Originally published in 1925, reprinted in 1969), pp. 99-100.

[22] Edward Eldefonso, Alan Coffey, and Richard C. Grace, *Principles of Law Enforcement* (New York: John Wiley & Sons, Inc., 1968), p. 121.

Soon other communities followed Los Angeles' example. By 1915 twenty-five cities had policewomen "paid from police appropriations." Chicago, with twenty-one, had the largest number.[23] Policewomen in Chicago had the following duties:[24]

1. The return of runaway girls to their homes.
2. The warning of young girls.
3. The suppression of dance hall evils.
4. The suppression of petty gambling in stores frequented by children.
5. The suppression of the sale of liquor to minors.
6. Service at railroad depots.
7. The conducting of investigations and the securing of evidence.

In 1915 policewomen earned between $800 and $1,200 per annum, substantially less than policemen. By the summer of that year, the International Association of Policewomen was organized in Baltimore. The objectives of the organization were threefold:[25]

1. To gather information as to the progress of policewomen's work and to furnish authentic data in response to inquiries from individuals and communities wishing to establish this work.
2. To maintain such a standard of character and efficiency as will attract to the work the highest type of women.
3. To advance general service to the community.

Incredibly, policewomen were striving for professionalism nearly four decades before most of their male counterparts progressed beyond the talking stage. In 1918 the Welfare Bureau of the New York City Police Department was placed under the direction of Mrs. Ellen O'Grady, who was given the rank of deputy police commissioner. Mrs. O'Grady was the first woman to be appointed to an executive position on an American police department. During the first six months of her command, Mrs. O'Grady's

[23] U. S. Census Bureau, *General Statistics of Cities* (1915), p. 18.

[24] *Supra* note 16, p. 228.

[25] *Ibid.*, pp. 232-233.

bureau handled 6,709 investigations.[26]

In 1919 Indianapolis created a Bureau of Policewomen. The Bureau handled over 5,000 cases in its first year of operation and won an enthusiastic commendation from its chief of police. That year, policewomen in Dayton, Ohio, persuaded city officials to establish and finance a Policewomen's House for misdemeanants and destitute females. A similar project was successfully under-taken in Seattle. By 1920 the International Association of Police-women was encouraging policewomen and policewoman can-didates to seek college-level training.

From 1910 to 1920 policewomen made substantial gains: pay began to improve; working conditions were bearable; they gained a measure of acceptance from their male colleagues; and of utmost importance, they rendered a needed service to the community. Over the years, the role of the policewoman was expanded to include a wide spectrum of police duties. Police honor roles contain the names of women who made outstanding contributions to their profession; some even made the ultimate sacrifice by forfeiting their lives to protect the community they had sworn to serve.

## THE EMERGENCE OF AMERICAN POLICE LITERATURE

The post-Civil War period saw the emergence of police liter-ature, an important intellectual development in the evolution of any craft, but especially important to an occupational group attempting to attain higher status in the eyes of the public, as many law enforcement agencies were trying to do. Foreign police scholars—especially those in England and France—began writing books on the subject of police administration, history, and reform before the close of the eighteenth century. By the third decade of the nineteenth century, a significant number of scholarly works had been produced by European authors, including Patrick Colquhoun and John Wade. But American law enforcement experienced an understandable lag in this area and it was late in the nineteenth century before a significant number of police books began appearing on the scene. However, when law enforce-ment literature began to appear, it did so in great profusion. Some of the most critically acclaimed works included *Police Records*

---

[26] *Semi-Annual Report of the Police Commissioner, New York City,* July 1, 1918, p. 27.

*and Recollections* (1873) by Edward H. Savage, a 240-year history of the Boston Police Department; Augustine Costello's *Our Police Protectors* (1885), a history of the New York Police Department from colonial times to the post-Civil War period; *The Philadelphia Police: Past and Present* (1887) by George W. Walling; George A. Tappan's *A 20th Century Souvenir: the Officers and Men of the Boston Police* (1901); Louis N. Robinson's *History and Organization of Criminal Statistics of the United States* (1911); *On the Enforcement of Law in Cities* (1913) by Brand Whitlock and *European Police Systems* (1915) by Raymond B. Fosdick.

Police scholars in the Gilded Age, admittedly a small group, provided the cornerstone for an American police literature. Slowly, almost painfully, it evolved until, in less than a century, it began to motivate a movement toward police professionalization and to provide a medium for education, self-examination, and reform.

### PIONEERS IN POLICE TRAINING

Although the most dramatic innovations in police training programs occurred in later eras, the foundation for those later developments was laid in the first two decades of the twentieth century by pioneering departments and individuals. The movement toward police training was motivated in no small measure by Raymond B. Fosdick, who, in his book *European Police Systems,* compared the efficiency of European and United States police forces, with the American police coming off decidedly second best.[27]

The first formal training school for policemen was established in Berkeley in 1908. The following year the New York City Police Department established a police academy, an outgrowth of its School of Pistol Practice which had been in operation since 1895.[28] Detroit established a training school for officers in 1911, while Philadelphia followed suit two years later. New York expanded the scope of its training to include detectives, also in

[27]V. A. Leonard, *Police Organization and Management* (Brooklyn: The Foundation Press, 1951), pp. 136-137.

[28]Allen Z. Gammage, *Police Training in the United States* (Springfield: Charles C Thomas, Publisher, 1963), p. 6.

1911.[29] In 1916 the University of California at Berkeley created the first training school for policemen in a university. Two years later the chief of police in Berkeley persuaded university officials to offer liberal arts courses for policemen, while the police department would teach technical police subjects. In 1918 the first school for policewomen was created at the University of California at Los Angeles.[30] California had clearly established itself as an early leader in the field of police training, a lead it has never relinquished.

## DEVELOPMENTS IN MUNICIPAL POLICING

Although the "big three" police departments—Boston, Philadelphia, and New York—led the way in implementing meaningful police reforms, they were joined by other emerging communities in instituting reforms and adopting new ideas. Just two years after Alexander Graham Bell invented the telephone, the Cincinnati Police Department installed a telephone exchange to serve the entire department, the first police agency in the country to completely replace the telegraph with the telephone. In 1881 Cincinnati organized a patrol wagon service, the second of its kind in the country. The department was reorganized in 1886: a detective unit was established; mounted policemen on horseback replaced foot patrolmen on outlying beats; an annual departmental inspection was inaugurated; a police library was placed in the headquarters building, and a system of awards was initiated to reward meritorious service in the ranks. By the second decade of the twentieth century, Cincinnati had created a traffic squad, replaced its horse patrol with automobiles and motorcycles, and established a criminal identification bureau.

In 1901 the Fitchburg, Massachusetts, Police Department was reorganized: a civil service system was implemented; patrol wagon service commenced; and the reserve police force, created five years earlier, was expanded. The department, following the lead of others, was organized along semimilitary lines. The following year a police ambulance service was initiated. In 1908 fifty-seven call

29*Supra* note 16, pp. 111-116.

30*Supra* note 29, pp. 60-62.

boxes and red lights were installed throughout the city. Several years later the city commissioned its first motorcycle detail.

One of the earliest police motorcycles, an Excelsior Autocycle, was used by the Detroit Police Department in 1915. Pedal to get rolling, then belt drive took over. *(Courtesy of the Detroit Police Department)*

The Flint, Michigan, Police Department appointed its first chief of police in 1890, replacing the earlier marshal system. Ten years later its first police station was built. In 1912 serious police reform began in Flint: the force was expanded to forty-four men; the department began furnishing uniforms and nightsticks to its officers, and the pay of policemen was doubled.

The Detroit Police Department established a juvenile unit in 1877, augmenting it with a truancy squad six years later. In 1897 bicycle patrolmen were added to the force. The Scorcher Cops, as they were known, were assigned almost exclusively to the apprehension of speeding bicycle riders, of which Detroit had its share. With the advent of the automobile, Detroit soon established itself as a leader in traffic safety innovations. Some of the Detroit Police

The world's first police car was a Detroit Police Model T Ford with home-made antenna. *(Courtesy of the Detroit Police Department)*

traffic safety firsts included: creation of the first "school safety patrol," installation of the first stop sign and the first automatic traffic signal light, formation of the first traffic school for violators, and the first use of pedestrian control by loudspeaker.

In 1895 uniforms were issued for the first time to officers in the Los Angeles Police Department. They were accompanied with an order from the chief of police to "keep your coats buttoned, stars pinned over left breast on outside of coat, and hold your clubs firmly," a bit of good advice for those early policemen. During the next ten years the Central Police Station was built, a police alarm system was installed, a bicycle squad was organized to patrol residential areas, and a new substation was opened. In the years immediately preceding World War I, a fingerprint repository was initiated and juvenile and identification bureaus were formed.

In 1905 *August Vollmer* was elected town marshal of Berkeley, a new California city. When the office of marshal was eliminated and replaced by the position of chief of police, Vollmer was appointed to the post, an appointment he held until 1932. Chief Vollmer was a gifted administrator who brought professional law

A traffic semaphore in the 1920s, operated by a Detroit patrolman. The Detroit Department was an early leader in developing and utilizing traffic safety devices. *(Courtesy of the Detroit Police Department)*

enforcement to Berkeley at a time when it was little more than a dream in other departments. Vollmer was instrumental in creating the first training school for policemen in Berkeley, and it was largely through his efforts that the University of California initiated its early criminology program. Police departments from across the country emulated Berkeley innovations, and the department served as a model for many agencies desiring internal reform. August Vollmer was to become the patriarch of California law enforcement and one of the most significant figures in the history of American policing. The Vollmer philosophy of municipal law enforcement consisted of twelve elements. Considering the stage of development of the American police, they were no less significant than the twelve tenets of Peelian reform:

1. The public is entitled to police service as efficient as budget and manpower permit.
2. Courtesy is of paramount importance in all public and private contacts with citizens.
3. Police personnel of the highest intelligence, good education, unquestioned integrity, and with a personal history demonstrating an ability to work in harmony with others

are necessary to effectively discharge the police responsibility.
4. Comprehensive, basic, advanced, and specialized training on a continuing basis is essential.
5. Broad responsibility should be assigned to the beat officer.
   Crime prevention through effective patrol.
   Investigation of all offenses.
   Traffic law enforcement.
   Juvenile duties.
   Public relations expert.
   Report writer.
   Thoroughly competent witness.
   A generalist rather than a specialist.
6. Superior supervision of personnel and effective leadership.
7. Good public relations in the broadest sense.
8. Cooperation with the press and news media.
9. Exemplary official and personal conduct.
10. Prompt investigation and disposition of personnel complaints.
11. Adherence to the law enforcement code of ethics.
12. Protection of individual rights while providing for the security of persons and property.

## THE VOLSTEAD ACT: LEGALLY ENFORCED ABSTINENCE

The attempts by certain groups to force—through legislative enactment by executive decree, or through moral suasion—communities to abstain from imbibing alcoholic beverages has been a recurring phenomenon in America, harking all the way back to colonial days. Many early groups spoke of "temperance" rather than outright "prohibition," choosing to persuade not legislate. It was not that those early groups did not want restrictive legislation; legislation was simply a politically impossible maneuver, so the old temperance societies chose preachment and promise of everlasting damnation to servants of "demon rum." But as the clamor against overindulgence grew, fragmented temperance organizations unified, became more militant, and a fullblown national movement evolved, one which abandoned the idea of temperance by persuasion and demanded abstinence by law.

The first great wave of prohibition began in 1846. Within ten

years, thirteen states had adopted laws prohibiting the manufacture, sale, or consumption of most types of alcoholic beverages.
By 1863, however, the wave receded as the number of prohibition
states had shrunk to five, four of which were southern states
which were to later secede from the union.[31]

Undismayed, the movement, made up of such groups as the
Prohibition Party, the Women's Christian Temperance Union
(WCTU), and the International Order of Good Templars (IOGT),
enlisted the aid of church groups and social service agencies, and
there was "a siege against the saloons."[32] By the 1880s another
wave of prohibition arrived, again to be short-lived. By 1913 the
prohibition movement was battle-scarred, but unbowed. Few
observers gave it an even outside chance for success, but an
unexpected factor was suddenly introduced into American life:
World War I.

The war accomplished three things for prohibitionists: (1) it
centralized authority in Washington, thus giving the national
government sweeping new powers to enact drastic legislation; (2)
it stressed the importance of saving food, making it appear
unpatriotic to "pour hundreds of millions of bushels of grain
annually into the breweries," and (3) it outlawed all things
German. As most brewers were German, it was an easy task for
prohibitionists to denounce them not only as enemies of temperance but as enemies of peace and the American way.[33] As the
Anti-Saloon League of New York stated:[34]

> The liquor traffic aids those forces in our country whose loyalty is called
> into question at this hour. The liquor traffic is the strong financial
> supporter of the German-American Alliance. The purpose of this Alliance
> is to secure German solidarity for the promotion of German ideals. . . .

With a new prestige gained through the war measures, disciples
of prohibition pressed hard for their goal. In October, 1919, after

---

[31]Charles Merz, *A Dry Decade* (Seattle: University of Washington Press, 1969), p. 3.

[32]Norman H. Clarke, *The Dry Years: Prohibition and Social Change in Washington* (Seattle: University of Washington Press, 1965), p. 29.

[33]*The New York Times,* June 18, 1917, p. 1.

[34]*Supra* note 32, p. 27.

years of trying, their efforts bore fruit when Congress passed, over President Wilson's veto, the drastic Volstead Act, which was later to be the Prohibition (Eighteenth) Amendment. The Act prohibited all liquor containing more than one half of one percent of alcohol. Prohibition had come.

## CONCLUSION

American law enforcement was entering a period of crisis. A law had been passed which significant numbers of people had not the slightest intention of obeying. Thrust into the untenable position of enforcing an unenforceable law, policemen were given the choice of exerting strong control over the country's drinking habits, or looking the other way as the public engaged in a socially acceptable vice. Some police departments followed the former course, others the latter. Too many police officials and politicians looked on prohibition as a way to give the public what it wanted—full access to speakeasies—while lining their pockets with payoff money received from illicit bars. Prohibition set the cause of police professionalization back decades. It has been said that prohibition was a "minus sum" game which produced no winners, only losers. But there was a winner created by legally enforced abstinence. In the late 1880s, the Italian population in many large American cities was terrorized by a group of foreign-born extortioners and racketeers. Prohibition was to convert these small time criminals into a powerful criminal syndicate whose evil influence was to spread across the country. The group was the Sicilian Society known as the Mafia.[35]

---

[35] Frank Shay, *Judge Lynch: His First Hundred Years* (Montclair, New Jersey: Patterson Smith Publishing Corp. Originally published in 1938, reprinted in 1969), p. 161.

In 1924 an unknown young attorney, John Edgar Hoover, was appointed Director of the troubled Federal Bureau of Investigation. Under Hoover's leadership, the FBI was to emerge as one of the most respected police agencies in the world. *(Courtesy of the FBI)*

*Chapter 7*

# POLICING PROHIBITION (1920-1929)

**P**rohibition, "the noble experiment that failed," should have worked. It had almost everything going for it, including a dry Constitution, a dry Congress, dry state legislatures, and support from a majority of the public. But it did not work because its supporters failed to take one factor into account: human frailty. There were individuals and groups who, for a price, worked diligently to fill the need created by this frailty. Whiskey literally poured across the border from Canada. It came in cars, in trucks, and in buses; it flowed through in planes and in boats; it gushed into cities by railroad car, in briefcases, in coat pockets, and in a hundred and one other ways. Whiskey that was not smuggled into the country was manufactured here in the thousands of unlawful stills that had popped up across the land. Bootlegging—the manufacture, sale, or transportation of illegal alcohol—became a big business, too big to remain disorganized. Gangs of all kinds and descriptions arose to form syndicates to capitalize on the demand for the illegal commodity.

Policing prohibition, even under the best of circumstances, would have been difficult. But the circumstances were far from ideal. The nation's police forces were generally badly paid, ill-trained, and poorly equipped. Many worked under the heavy hand of domineering politicians who had entered into collusive relationships with gangsters to thwart, rather than suppress, liquor law violations. Those agencies that honestly tried to enforce prohibition, including the Federal Government, did so in a rather swashbuckling and self-defeating manner. Prohibition inaugurated the most extensive effort ever undertaken to legally change the social habits of an entire nation. Consequently, it would have been reasonable to expect that the enforcement of such a unique enterprise would have been launched carefully, with specially selected and trained police forces whose enforcement efforts would be tempered toward enlisting public support and aid. No such course of action was followed. Thousands of small consumers were arrested while large dealers pursued their business with little interference, thus antagonizing the very people whose support the police vitally needed. There was much effort to accomplish by force what could be accomplished only by suasion. There was no recognizable pattern of enforcement. Some communities moved vigorously to enforce all violations of the new law, while others proceeded on a more selective course. Some agencies concentrated on arresting consumers, while others focused their efforts on producers and suppliers. Still others took a permissive attitude toward the entire law, overlooking all violations, both major and minor. This latter attitude was generally motivated by economics, not altruism.

On the Federal level, three agencies were charged with the enforcement of prohibition: The Bureau of Internal Revenue, the Customs Bureau, and the United States Coast Guard. The supervision of these agencies was placed in the hands of an Assistant Secretary of the Treasury. Five persons held that office between 1920 and 1925, and for a period of five months the office was vacant. Federal enforcement agents were appointed without the protection of civil service, a situation which lent itself to corruption. Agents in the field were supervised by state directors, forty-eight in all. From 1921 to 1925, 184 men were in and out of

This armored car was a familiar sight in Detroit during prohibition as it sallied forth to meet the enemy—bootleggers. *(Courtesy of the Detroit Police Department)*

those forty-eight positions.[1] It was little wonder that the Federal Government experienced little success in policing prohibition.

## THE NEW CRIME SITUATION

Prohibition had an accelerating influence on crime. New classes of crime and criminality were created and some traditional crimes took on new significance because of the intensity and frequency with which they were increasingly being committed. Adding to the crime problem was the automobile, which was becoming a weapon (e.g. gangland slayings), an accomplice (e.g. bank robberies), and a victim (e.g. auto thefts). Police, spread thin because of prohibition, were almost helpless to do anything about the rapidly rising crime rate. The trend of crime was upward and the newness of it all baffled even the experts.

### Organized Crime

The demand for a particular product—intoxicating liquor—coupled with the failure of society to provide lawful means for satisfying the demand created crime organizations of mammoth proportions. Underworld empires based on beer and liquor flourished. The open flaunting of the law by millions of otherwise honest citizens even gave the new crime lords an aura of respectability. Bootleggers were often looked upon as professional men in the same social class as physicians, attorneys, and bankers. Gangs arose to organize the early fragmented liquor trade, and before long even the smallest operators owed allegiance to some type of organization. Gangs were usually classified in three ways:[2]

**The Neighborhood Play Group.** Neighborhood play groups, or social clubs, had existed in large cities well before prohibition. They held neighborhood dances; sponsored picnics, clambakes, and bank concerts; gave parties, and built clubhouses for fraternal activities. In some neighborhoods everyone who was anyone was a member of the neighborhood

[1] The National Commission on Law Observance and Enforcement, *Preliminary Report on Prohibition,* Vol. 1 (Washington: U.S. Government Printing Office, 1931), p. 13.

[2] The Illinois Association for Criminal Justice, *The Illinois Crime Survey* (Montclair, New Jersey: Patterson Smith Publishing Corp. Originally published in 1929, reprinted in 1968), pp. 1001-1015.

social club. When the Volstead Act was passed, many formerly legitimate groups turned their activities to the illicit liquor trade, not for profit but for their own use, a main function of clubs being to allow members to drink in a congenial atmosphere. Later, however, the lure of big money motivated a large number of neighborhood play groups to enter the illegal trade for a profit. Social clubs were actually converted into organized criminal gangs within short periods of time. The transformation of a Chicago amateur baseball team called the Ragen Colts was in many ways typical of the evil metamorphosis that changed legal community organizations into extralegal crime syndicates. The Colts was a rather good baseball team at the turn of the century. Later it became an athletic club which sponsored neighborhood sporting events of all kinds, along with annual picnics and minstrel shows. Gradually, as politicians and prospective office holders sought out its leaders for help in seeking public office, the club assumed a more political stance. When prohibition came, the activities of the Colts were predictable. They entered the illegal beer business, hired themselves out as strongarm men and actually gunned down rivals in the beer business. From baseball team to mob in less than twenty years.

**The Ethnic Gang.** Even before prohibition small-time criminal gangs had existed in large cities. These gangs differed from neighborhood play groups in that they were formed for the business administration of crime. Most had an ethnic flavor. Early gangs engaged in terror tactics—bombings, assaults, and threats of violence—in order to extort money from frightened merchants. Extortion letters often contained the mark of the Black Hand, the symbol of a secret Sicilian society. Prohibition created a fertile ground for these ethnic gangs, and small mobs were converted into massive crime syndicates which gripped cities in an iron fist. The Al Capone Gang was probably the best example of an ethnic gang which, through a combination of skill and brutality, arose to control the vice of one of the nation's largest cities, Chicago. Before Capone went to jail for income tax evasion in 1931, it was charged that he had more than 1,000 gunmen on his payroll.

**The Professional Gang.** Professional gangs had basically the same goals as ethnic gangs; however, they were generally feudal groups whose members were of many nationalities. Chicago's Dion O'banion Gang was a professional organization which recruited its members from the ranks of skilled criminal craftsmen: safe-crackers, armed robbers, and successful burglars. O'banion took over and organized the vice of a section of Chicago. He was not destined to survive, though. Internal problems and the competition from the Capone Gang were to prematurely end his business enterprise and his life.

The emergence of a *professional* class of criminals led to intergang rivalries that stunned the country and focused the attention of the world on American lawlessness. Bloody gang wars were waged on the streets of cities; policemen were shot down as they walked their beats, and the blasts of bombs and the burst of machine gun fire became familiar city sounds. In Chicago a total of 257 gangland murders occurred between 1923 and 1929. During 1926 and 1927 Cook County, Illinois, had 130 gang murders, none of which was solved.[3] Public patience with the gangster era ended when in 1929 one group of hoodlums, purported to be from Al Capone's gang, machine gunned to death seven hoodlums of a rival mob in a garage on Chicago's North Side. This, the Saint Valentine's Day Massacre, prompted some thirty retaliatory gang murders that year and polarized citizen opinion against gangsterism.[4]

## Auto Theft

The problem of auto theft was created the day the automobile was invented. Although cars were stolen from the time they first hit the nation's streets, the development of speedy, streamlined autos, mass-produced in great numbers, caused a virtual wave of auto thefts. In 1918 the nation's twenty-eight largest cities reported about 27,000 auto thefts. Within ten years, this number had increased to nearly 100,000.[5] Few crimes pointed up the

[3]The Citizens' Police Committee, *Chicago Police Problems* (Montclair, New Jersey: Patterson Smith Publishing Corp. Originally published in 1931, reprinted in 1969), pp. 3-4.

[4]John Lofton, *Justice and the Press* (Boston: Beacon Press, 1966), pp. 100-101.

[5]August Vollmer, *The Police and Modern Society* (Berkeley: University of California Press, 1936), p. 59.

growing helplessness of the local police better than auto theft. Thieves' operations were not limited to specifically defined political boundaries, although the police were virtual prisoners within their jurisdictions, with little coordination or cooperation between departments. Furthermore, auto theft was a relatively new crime and law enforcement agencies had little experience with the phenomenon. Municipal and state governments passed laws against automobile thefts; however, they soon discovered that cars were stolen for varying reasons. Consequently, by the mid-1920s, multiple laws dealing with auto thefts were passed which dealt not only with the actual theft but also with the intent of the thief. The three most prevalent forms of auto theft were the following:

**Joy Riding.** Whereby a vehicle was used without the consent of its owner, but with no intent to permanently deprive him of his car. This offense was committed primarily by young people in need of transportation.

**Auto Theft.** The crime of auto theft generally referred to a professional offense committed by one who had the intention of altering and reselling the car or stripping it of parts. Expert theft rings shipped cars all over the world. Some thieves even purchased automobile dealerships as an outlet for their stolen stock.

**Auto Theft as a Crime Tool.** Possibly the most dangerous type of theft was perpetrated by those criminals in need of a fast getaway car to use during armed robberies. Some robbers hatched elaborate plots to stash stolen getaway cars at different locations, baffling pursuing peace officers.

## Kidnapping

Kidnapping for ransom was not an invention of the 1920s. The earliest recorded kidnapping had occurred in Philadelphia in 1874 when four-year-old Charley Ross was abducted and held for ransom.[6] But like so many other crimes, the incidents of kidnapping peaked during the twenties and early thirties. Again, like other crimes, it was successful, at least at first, because of the inability of the police to cope with it. Kidnappings in the pro-

[6]George A. Walling, *Recollections of a New York Chief of Police* (Montclair, New Jersey: Patterson Smith Publishing Corp. Originally published in 1890, reprinted in 1969).

hibition era aroused public concern because of the consistency with which the victims were killed. The most sensational case occurred in 1924 when Nathan Leopold and Richard Loeb, two wealthy youths, kidnapped and killed fourteen-year-old Bobby Franks for no apparent reason. The Leopold-Loeb case was front-page news for months. If one positive thing came from the case, it was that it galvanized public opinion against such acts, thus motivating new laws and modern methods of communication to combat the problem. Eight years after the Leopold-Loeb case, the infant son of flyer Charles A. Lindbergh was kidnapped and killed, prompting additional legislative action in this area.

## Armed Robbery

Many police administrators of the day blamed the alarming increase in armed robberies during the 1920s on the ready availability of high-powered guns and automobiles. The old "slugger" who pursued his calling with a lead pipe or blackjack was replaced by the masked holdup man wielding a submachine gun and driving a black Packard Sedan. By 1925 America was experiencing 125,000 holdups a year. Due to the lucrative nature of the crime, former pickpockets, burglars, and forgers armed themselves and changed occupations. No gas station, mail truck, bank, bar, restaurant, or store was safe from the new breed of "stickup man." Everything from Fort Knox to the corner grocery store was a prospective target.[7]

### EMPIRICAL INQUIRY INTO POLICE ACTIVITY

High crime rates, gangsterism, violent individual and collective antisocial behavior, coupled with the obvious inability of the police to effectively deal with these problems, led to considerable public concern with American law enforcement. The country was riding the crest of a crime wave of epidemic proportions and the police appeared powerless to combat it. Citizen concern prompted many communities to create *ad hoc* commissions to scrutinize the police problem—and in some cases, crime and the criminal justice system—for the purpose of recommending a remedy for the malaise. More than one-hundred surveys into crime and the break-

---

[7]*Supra* note 5, pp. 28-34.

down of policing were conducted during the decade. America has a tradition of empirical inquiry into police activity. That tradition began in the prohibition era.[8]

In 1920 six prominent attorneys—including Roscoe Pound and Felix Frankfurter—formed a committee under the auspices of the National Popular Government League, a private organization, to investigate the law enforcement practices of the United States Department of Justice. The committee's findings hardly instilled confidence in Federal law enforcement. According to the committee, Justice Department agents consistently made searches and arrests without warrants; inflicted corporal punishment on suspected criminals; planted agent provocateurs in radical political organizations; compelled, through terror tactics, persons to be witnesses against themselves, and propagandized against radical groups in order to enlist public support for the department's harassment activities.[9]

In 1912 the Cleveland Bar Association requested the Cleveland Foundation to conduct a massive survey of the city's criminal justice system—the police, the criminal courts, the bar, and correctional institutions. The Foundation undertook the task and found waste, inefficiency, duplication of effort, some corruption, overburdened courts, crowded jail facilities, and a generally poor quality of police manpower. The Foundation's findings were not just an indictment of law enforcement in Cleveland, but a critique of the general system of American policing:[10]

> Police machinery in the United States has not kept pace with modern demands. It has developed no effective technique to master the burden which modern social and industrial conditions impose. Clinging to old traditions, bound by old practices which business and industry long ago discarded, employing a personnel poorly adapted to its purpose, it grinds away on its perfunctory task without self criticism, without imagination, and with little initiative.

[8]Delmar Karlen, *Anglo-American Criminal Justice* (New York: Oxford University Press, 1967), pp. 98-99.

[9]National Popular Government League, *Report Upon the Illegal Practices of the U.S. Department of Justice* (New York: Arno Press. Originally published in 1920, reprinted in 1969).

[10]The Cleveland Foundation, *Criminal Justice in Cleveland* (Montclair, New Jersey: Patterson Smith Publishing Corp. Originally published in 1926, reprinted in 1969), p. 5.

In 1926 a group of civic organizations formed the Illinois Association for Criminal Justice. After its inception, a study was conducted of organized crime in the state, the police, and the machinery of justice. With regard to the police, the Association reached the following conclusion:[11]

> The fundamental cause of the demoralization of the police. . .is corrupt political influence, the departments being dominated and controlled for years by such influence. Until the condition is removed, there is little hope for any substantial betterment.

In 1928 a special Grand Jury was convened in Chicago to investigate crime in Cook County. What it uncovered was the tip of an iceberg of graft and corruption. A three-cornered alliance between politicians, the police, and gangsters was exposed. The Grand Jury declared that the Chicago Police Department was "rotten to the core," a bit of an overstatement but one which reflected the depth to which the department had fallen in the eyes of the citizenry.[12]

In 1929 President Herbert Hoover announced the appointment of the National Commission on Law Observance and Enforcement, consisting of eleven members, with former United States Attorney General George W. Wickersham as chairman. The Commission was to take two years to complete its work; however, it fulfilled its task well and in 1931 the most comprehensive criminal justice survey in the country's history was handed to the President. It is discussed in the following chapter.

## IN RESPONSE TO CRITICISM

The police establishment was stung by the barrage of criticism which had been leveled at it from the survey commissions. Some police officials tried to defend themselves and their departments against charges of corruption and inefficiency, but most commissions had done their work well and indictments were painstakingly documented. While the criticism did not motivate a revolution in law enforcement, certain substantial reforms and modifications were undertaken by police agencies desirous of upgrading themselves.

[11]*Supra* note 3, p. 372.

[12]*Supra* note 3, p. 3.

In the private sector the National Automobile Theft Bureau was created by the insurance industry to maintain a national clearing house for stolen car information. The Bureau, headquartered in New York City, was staffed with highly trained investigators whose job it was to track down large auto-theft rings. A federal law prohibiting the interstate transportation of stolen cars gave the Bureau and the police a needed tool to combat the illegal business.

In 1924 the Justice Department appointed a young attorney, John Edgar Hoover, to direct the Federal Bureau of Investigation. Hoover completely reorganized the FBI, divorcing it from politics and starting it on the road toward professionalization. Within eleven years, Director Hoover had established an identification division as a national clearing house for criminal fingerprint records, formed a technical laboratory to aid in the investigation of cases, created a training school for newly appointed special agents, and founded a national academy which offered agent training to municipal, county, and state law enforcement officers. The FBI was given expanded jurisdiction by a Congress which began passing new laws at an unprecedented rate. The FBI's additional duties led to an increasingly hazardous situation for agents, who in 1934 were empowered to carry firearms.

The enforcement of prohibition also underwent some modification. A Prohibition Bureau was organized within the Treasury Department, and during President Herbert Hoover's administration, a change in philosophy was implemented. Agents were given public relations training to motivate them to "act always as gentlemen."[13] The Bureau's emphasis was placed on detecting and capturing large liquor dealers rather than small-time consumers. A policy on the use of firearms was adopted because of previous incidents of weapon misuse by agents. Prohibition agents were ordered to abandon dramatic raids aimed at making sensational headlines and concentrate on enforcing the law in a quiet, orderly manner. In 1929 Eliot Ness was appointed head of the Prohibition Bureau. Ness was a competent and dedicated administrator whose enforcement efforts were loosely depicted in a later television show entitled "The Untouchables."

The prohibition era saw a movement toward meaningful educa-

---

[13]*The New York Times,* April 23, 1929.

tional programs for policemen, although the decade was more a period of experimentation than anything else. In 1923 the University of California at Berkeley granted the first baccalaureate degree to a student with a minor in criminology. The recipient, a Berkeley police officer, was probably the first man in the country to be awarded a college degree in a course of study which included technical police subjects. In 1925 Harvard University established the Bureau of Street Traffic Research in the Graduate School. In 1929 the University of Chicago inserted a police training program into the school's regular curriculum. The curriculum stressed courses in police administration. Although the program was short-lived, it was the first time in history that technical police training courses were integrated into a regular, undergraduate curriculum.[14]

### THE DEPRESSION'S EFFECT ON THE POLICE

Municipal law enforcement, the recipient of most of the criticism aimed at criminal justice agencies, was also quick to react to public disapproval. The Chicago Police Department organized "flying squads" to speed to the scene of crimes and begin immediate investigations. The city purchased a fleet of thirty-six high-powered automobiles for that purpose. A staff of 250 detectives was assigned to the state attorney's office. The department also tried to end its discriminatory liquor law arrest procedure by forming a "dress suit squad" to apprehend "exclusive society violators of the law."

In 1924 Philadelphia, in response to citizen outrage over crime conditions, appointed as Director of Public Safety a United States Marine Corps Brigadier-General, Smedley D. Butler. During his second week in office, over 2,000 people were arrested for violating the prohibition laws and more than 1,000 saloons were closed. A wholesale reorganization of the department was undertaken, and eight lieutenants were suspended for dereliction of duty. General Butler invited the city's 1,600 firemen to "pitch-in and help enforce the law."

Many police agencies paid a heavy price for professionalizing.

[14]Allen Z. Gammage, *Police Training in the United States* (Springfield: Charles C Thomas, Publisher, 1963), pp. 62-64.

Berkeley Police Sergeant "Bumpy" Lee *(left)* and Officer Ralph Proctor *(right)* survey the intersection of Bancroft Way and Telegraph Avenue. Across the street is the campus of the University of California. *(Courtesy of the Berkeley Police Department)*

Police deaths reached a new high in the decade. In Kansas City alone twenty-six officers were killed in the line of duty from 1920-1929.

During the 1920s the Los Angeles Police Department underwent broad changes: standards for personnel were elevated; the training program was lengthened and intensified; a building program resulted in badly needed precinct stations; specialized technicians, such as research chemists and ballistics experts, were hired, and a pistol range was built.

Detroit, in an effort to place policemen where they were most needed, opened and staffed seven new precinct stations. A full radio system was operationalized in patrol cars.

The New Orleans Police Department initiated a medical training program for its officers and in 1922 received a national award for being the only force in the country fully equipped to administer first aid to citizens.

In 1928 Orlando W. Wilson was appointed Chief of Police of Wichita. O. W. Wilson was to establish himself as one of the nation's most distinguished police administrators and scholars, a man whose name was to become synonymous with dedication, honesty, and enlightened leadership. Under Wilson's eleven-year reign, the Wichita Police Department experienced a total rejuvenation: officers were encouraged to seek college-level training;

entry standards were uplifted; a police academy was initiated; record-keeping procedures were reorganized; foot patrolmen, an expensive proposition, were reassigned to patrol cars for maximum manpower efficiency; a junior traffic squad, made up of school children, was organized, and principles of sound management and administration were strengthened at all levels of the department.

In 1928 Cincinnati created a centralized bureau of records, and a new system of crime classification was established in conjunction with the International Association of Chiefs of Police. The system was so successful that it was used as a model for the FBI's *Uniform Crime Reports,* thus establishing the Cincinnati Police Department as a pioneer in the field of modern police records.

### CONCLUSION

The history of law enforcement in the 1920s may be viewed by the iconoclast in a totally negative context; as a history replete with police corruption, patronage, nepotism, graft, brutality, and collusive involvements with gangsters. But to assume that the most dramatic historical machinations of the era were also the most significant is to come away with a distorted appraisal of an institution upon which conflicting and often impossible demands were made. It is not historically significant that large numbers of policemen became grafters, that many command officers were corrupt, that crime became organized, and that criminals ruled cities. Under the political and social circumstances that existed in the 1920s, it would have been difficult to expect otherwise. What was truly significant about the era was that with all the pressures to sell out to the corruptors, a dedicated group of policemen bucked the tide of corruption and made substantial contributions to their craft, to their departments, to their communities, and to their country. The twenties produced both the corruptor and the corrupted, but it also produced a breed of incorruptable men and women whose accomplishments stand out for all to view.

Orlando W. Wilson, Chief of the Wichita Police Department and one of the most respected names in the history of American law enforcement.

*Chapter 8*

# THE THIRTIES: A NEW DEAL FOR THE POLICE (1930-1939)

S oaring crime rates, rampant gangsterism, police corruption, and the open and flagrant flaunting of the law by otherwise honest citizens convinced many Americans that prohibition was simply not worth the price that the country was paying. By the end of the 1920s, Al Capone had built an empire which was grossing 60 million dollars per year, an empire which had diversified into gambling, labor unions, and laundries. When in October of 1929 the Wall Street crash plunged the nation into a depression, groups of citizens banded together in organizations to work for the repeal of the Eighteenth Amendment, reasoning that an end to prohibition would lower taxes and bring prosperity to the land. Two years later the growing movement for repeal was to receive strong backing when the Wickersham Commission completed its investigation and released its findings.

## THE WICKERSHAM COMMISSION REPORTS

In 1931 the National Commission on Law Observance and Enforcement reported that prohibition was not being enforced because basically it was unenforceable. But the Commission went far beyond an analysis of prohibition. In what a newspaper of the era called "the most astonishing document ever submitted to our government by a responsible committee," the Wickersham Commission released fourteen volumes which probed deeply into the entire machinery of American criminal justice. Two of the reports directly concerned the police: *Report Number 11—Lawlessness in Law Enforcement* and *Report Number 14—The Police.* Neither was particularly complimentary. The police had been found to be using third-degree methods—physical and psychological torture—to extract confessions from suspects. Furthermore, it was reported that (1) police corruption was widespread and training was almost non-existent; (2) inefficiency was the rule rather than the exception; (3) communications systems were ineffective; (4) political interference in police operations hampered honest enforcement efforts, and (5) police executives were often ill-suited to handle their jobs. The Commission cited one example of a big city mayor appointing his tailor to the position of chief of police "because he had been his tailor for twenty years and he knew he was a good tailor and so necessarily would make a good chief of police."[1] American law enforcement was not entirely without its bright lights, however, as the Commission found a number of police departments which were superior in every respect. Milwaukee was cited as a relatively "crime free" city where criminals were speedily detected, arrested, tried, and convicted. The Commission reflected that Milwaukee's success was largely due to the continuity of police command; the police department had had but two chiefs in forty-six years. The Detroit Police Department was commended for its efficient use of the police radio, an efficiency which had resulted in a phenomenal arrest rate.[2] But American policing, despite the shining accomplishments of a few agencies, was still badly in need of reform and the report on the police prepared by August Vollmer and political scientists David G. Monroe and Earle W. Garrett among others, made ten recommendations relating to the police:[3]

1. The corrupting influence of politics should be removed from the police organization.
2. The head of the department should be selected at large for competence, a leader, preferably a man of considerable police experience, and removable from office only after preferment of charges and a public hearing.
3. Patrolmen should be able to rate a "B" on the Alpha Test, be able-bodied and of good character, weigh 150 pounds, measure 5 feet 9 inches tall, and be between 21 and 31 years of age. These requirements may be disregarded by the chief for good and sufficient reasons.

---

[1]National Commission on Law Observance and Enforcement, *Report on the Police* (Montclair, New Jersey: Patterson Smith Publishing Corp. Originally published in 1931, reprinted in 1968), p. 3.

[2]*Ibid.,* p. 5.

[3]*Ibid.,* p. 140.

4. Salaries should permit decent living standards, housing should be adequate, eight hours of work, one day off weekly, annual vacation, fair sick leave with pay, just accident and death benefits when in performance of duty, reasonable pension provisions on an actuarial basis.
5. Adequate training for recruits, officers, and those already on the roll is imperative.
6. The communication system should provide for call boxes, telephones, recall system, and teletype and radio.
7. Records should be complete, adequate, but as simple as possible. They should be used to secure administrative control of investigations and of department units in the interest of efficiency.
8. A crime prevention unit should be established if circumstances warrant this action, and qualified women police should be engaged to handle juvenile delinquents' and women's cases.
9. State police forces should be established in states where rural protection of this character is required.
10. State bureaus of criminal investigation and information should be established in every state.

For the first time in history American law enforcement had a set of guidelines on which to base reform efforts and technological improvements. Over the years students of law enforcement have relied heavily on the Wickersham Commission Reports as a source of scholarly material. The positive impact of the National Commission on Law Observance and Enforcement on the police craft has been immeasurable.

## THE MARCH TOWARD PROGRESS

Spurred by the Wickersham Reports, the police entered a time of real progress. Prohibition, mercifully, was repealed, thereby eliminating one problem with which the police had been grappling. Municipal police departments began to professionalize their operations, furnished by Wickersham with the model to do so and the ammunition to motivate politicians to permit internal reform and the adoption of technological innovations.

Police departments moved quickly to minimize the influence of external politics and to upgrade working conditions for sworn personnel. In 1931 the Detroit Police Department initiated a new system for the selection of personnel. Before the decade was over, a merit promotion system was to be installed. Within months after the release of the findings of the Wickersham Commission, the

Cincinnati Police Department created an improved retirement system. In 1935 the police credit union was formed, one of the first in the country. In 1931 the Tucson Police Department was placed under civil service, lessening to a great degree the political interference which had for years hampered the cause of professional law enforcement in that city.

Advanced technology made its imprint on police departments. In 1931 sophisticated systems of radio communications were established in scores of cities, including Kansas City, New Orleans, and Cincinnati. In 1934 Cincinnati created one of the most modern crime laboratories in the country, equipped with ballistics equipment, x-ray, a polygraph (first used by the Berkeley Police Department), moulage, and other equipment. In 1935 the Kansas City Police Department installed two-way radios in patrol cars, and each car was equipped with the new familiar "whip" antenna.

Police departments also began to experiment with innovative administrative techniques. Emulating business and the military, many departments for the first time initiated principles of sound management. In 1936 August Vollmer published *The Police and Modern Society,* a major work in the field of police administration and one which for years served as a classic text that police com-

During the gangster era, policemen found it necessary to adopt advanced weaponry and high-powered automobiles. *(Courtesy of the Columbus, Ohio, Police Department)*

mand officers and executives consulted in modifying the structure and function of their agencies. Typical of the new emphasis on sound administrative techniques, the state of Texas reorganized its state police by creating a Department of Public Safety to unify fragmented state law enforcement agencies, including the Texas Rangers. In New Orleans the system of dual control of police operations was eliminated and the responsibility for managing the department was lodged in a supervisor of police. In 1939 the San Antonio Police Department was completely reorganized by Chief Ray Ashworth. Chief Ashworth devised a system of organization which is virtually intact to this day.

Probably the most significant developments in law enforcement during the 1930s occurred in the dual fields of police training and education. By the end of the decade every state, with the exception of Wisconsin, had created a state police force. These early state forces led the way in implementing progressive training programs, most of which were at least three months in duration. The first state police academy was established in New York, with Pennsylvania quickly following suit. By 1934 state police schools had been established in Michigan, New Jersey, Connecticut, Oregon, Washington, and Texas.[4] The impact of these early schools cannot be overstated, for they motivated municipal departments to implement training programs of their own, although municipal training programs were to lag sadly behind their state counterparts. The state police were to take up some of the slack by permitting, on a limited basis, selected municipal policemen to attend state training academies. The FBI also had a significant influence on municipal law enforcement when in 1935 it created the National Academy for the training of local police officers. In the early thirties, Northwestern University established the Northwestern Traffic Safety Institute—a two-week traffic course, under the direction of Frank M. Kreml. In 1935 Northwestern's program—which over the years was to become one of the most distinguished of its kind—was expanded to include three courses: one for local policemen, one for state officers, and an advanced course for graduates of the basic program.[5]

---

[4]Allen Z. Gammage, *Police Training in the United States* (Springfield: Charles C Thomas, Publisher, 1963), pp. 10-16.

[5]*Ibid.*, p. 19.

In the field of police education, San Jose State College established the first complete police major program in the country in 1931. The following year August Vollmer was appointed Professor of Police Administration at the University of California at Berkeley, where he drafted a curriculum which, for the first time in history, allowed students to major in either the technical, legal, or social areas of policing and obtain an A.B. degree with a major in criminology. In 1935 the first police cadet program in American history was created when O. W. Wilson's Wichita Police Department agreed to hire annually fourteen University of Wichita upper-division students. The students worked part-time for the police department—for pay—while pursuing their education at the university. Graduates, who took both technical police subjects and academic courses, received an A. B. in political science. Many sought employment with the Wichita Police Department upon graduation. That same year, Michigan State College (later to become Michigan State University) established a four-year program leading to a B. S. in police administration. The program was eventually to be housed in the School of Police Administration and Public Safety. It has become one of the largest and most respected police programs in the country. Before the decade was over, more than twenty colleges and universities were to begin offering police training programs of one sort or another.[6]

## THE DEPRESSION'S EFFECT ON THE POLICE

The Depression had a devastating effect on America: millions were jobless; people who had never before experienced economic problems were homeless; the economy sank lower and lower. Yet the phenomenon created few problems for the police. There were few signs of social disruption, even though communists constantly agitated for revolution with no success. In fact, outbursts of collective violence were minimal, the notable exception occurring in 1932 when World War I Veterans rioted in Washington in protest over the government's refusal to pay them a bonus for wartime service.

The Depression had a positive impact on police operations in two ways. First, during the Depression police departments were able to recruit from a population which, for the first time,

[6]*Ibid.,* pp. 64-72.

included many unemployed college graduates. People who under normal conditions would not have given a second thought to entering the police service now stood in employment lines in hopes that they could win a patrolman's appointment. New blood was infused into law enforcement agencies badly in need of such a transfusion. For years municipal departments made good use of this newly found manpower bonanza. As general economic conditions improved, however, the police job became less and less attractive and many college graduates left the service to seek more gainful employment. Little provision had been made to financially attract and keep college-educated policemen; so when the Depression's effects began to ease, wholesale resignation of college graduates were forthcoming. But some stayed on, men who found that the rewards they received from policing far transcended the material satisfactions that they could have received in business or industry. Although relatively small in number, this group of dedicated, well-educated men were to assume roles of trust and responsibility on police departments and, some decades hence, were to spearhead a movement to professionalize the nation's police.

Second, the New Deal, President Franklin Delano Roosevelt's answer to the Depression, had as one of its goals the employment of large numbers of people. Accordingly, the Works Progress Administration (WPA) was created to "help men keep their chins up and their hands in," a task it fulfilled by embarking on a massive construction program. The WPA, among other projects, built or rebuilt over 110,000 public buildings.[7] Law enforcement reaped wholesale benefits from this program. New police stations were constructed; older buildings were renovated. Special facilities, such as firing ranges, substations, jails, maintenance garages, and police academies, which would not otherwise have been built for decades, were among WPA projects.

The social problems of the Depression were national in scope, so it was only logical that the solutions for them would come from Washington. Accordingly, the Federal Government assumed sweeping new authority, passing legislation and assuming control over matters which, during other times, would have been

---

[7]Richard N. Current, T. Harry Williams, and Frank Friedel, *American History: A Survey* (New York: Alfred A. Knopf, 1964), p. 740.

thoroughly opposed by local and state governments. But this was an extraordinary time and extraordinary measures were needed. Local reliance on the Federal Government to solve social and economic problems led to a similar reliance on Washington to solve the crime problem. As a result, the FBI was thrust into a crime-fighting role which had previously been filled by municipal police departments.

## THE FBI AND CONTEMPORARY DESPERADOES

The Depression saw the rise of a new kind of American outlaw—one who was in many ways similar to the lawless element that had terrorized the Old West a half-century previously, but who, by the very nature of the tools of his trade, was different and a hundred times more deadly. Instead of horses, these contemporary desperadoes drove high-powered cars. Instead of six-shooters, their basic tool was the submachine gun. In place of stage coaches and trains, they robbed armored cars and banks. Small bands of desperadoes roamed the country almost at will, holding up banks, kidnapping tellers, shooting down guards, policemen, or anyone else who stood in the way of a successful job. One of the most notorious contemporary outlaws was John Dillinger, bank robber and murderer. In September, 1931, Dillinger was arrested by local authorities and jailed in Lima, Ohio. Less than one month later Dillinger, assisted by his confederates, broke jail and killed the sheriff. After a three-month orgy of murder and robbery, he was apprehended in Arizona and lodged in Crown Point, Indiana's "escape-proof" jail. He escaped within the month, leaving the state in a stolen sheriff's car. With an estimated five thousand policemen in pursuit, Dillinger (1) stopped for a haircut in a barber shop, (2) bought getaway cars, (3) enjoyed a home-cooked dinner with his family in his home town, and (4) burglarized a police station, relieving it of arms and ammunition. Dillinger's exploits pointed up, once again, the impotence of the local police in dealing with violent interstate crimes and criminals. The Dillinger episode prompted the Federal authorities to act. The FBI was granted expanded enforcement powers and ordered to end the reign of terror of the latter-day outlaws. The FBI was remarkably efficient in doing just that. In July, 1934, John Dillinger was killed by agents as he left a theatre in Chicago. Three months later Pretty Boy Floyd was shot down in East Liverpool, Ohio. The following month Baby Face Nelson, Public Enemy Number One, was killed in a shootout with agents near Niles Center, Illinois. The FBI and J. Edgar Hoover became heroes to a nation in the throes of a depression and badly in need of heroes. The success of the FBI prompted Congress to pass a whole list of new Federal crimes, including kidnapping and robbery of banks insured by the Federal Deposit Insurance Corporation.[8]

## CONCLUSION

Municipal police forces began making significant progress in the thirties. Salaries were improved, political influence was eased, new equipment was adopted, modern facilities were built, and old structures were renovated. Some police departments (e.g. Berkeley, Cincinnati, and Wichita) were true models, shining examples of what law enforcement agencies ought to be like. But a lingering problem persisted even in this era of progress. What the American police service needed more than any technical or administrative innovation was manpower—superior manpower. When the Depression forced an army of qualified personnel to seek employment on police departments, municipal governments failed to respond by significantly upgrading salaries and fringe benefits to a point where they were competitive with the private sector, and the army was whittled to a platoon by Depression's end. The decade saw the Federal Government adopt broad new powers to end the Depression. A corresponding increase in Federal powers was aimed at solving the nation's crime problem. Accordingly, the role of the FBI was expanded. Police agencies were beginning to move toward professionalization, but a dread social phenomenon was to interrupt the journey—war.

[8]William E. Leuchtenburg, *Franklin D. Roosevelt and the New Deal* (New York: Harper and Row, Publishers, Inc., 1963), p. 334.

Tracer bullets being fired from machine guns by special agents of the FBI during night firearms training. *(Courtesy of the FBI)*

## Chapter 9

# THE WAR YEARS AND AFTER (1940-1949)

**A**ny substantial change in the social environment of the country has a direct effect on law enforcement. Economic crises, labor disputes, technological advancements, breakthroughs in methods of transportation and communication, new legislation, and foreign immigration all had a significant impact on the structure and function of American policing. Anything that affects the nation in a dramatic way also affects the police. When in the early 1940s the United States entered World War II, special problems—both internal and external—were created for the police.

### THE POLICE GO TO WAR

During World War II the ranks of local and state police agencies were seriously depleted as tens of thousands of officers went off to war. The war may well have been law enforcement's finest hour to date. Policemen abroad distinguished themselves in battle, but they paid a heavy price. More than a few police stations contain plaques honoring the department's war dead. At home the shortage in qualified manpower created the need for extraordinary measures.

A Civilian Defense Corps was established to perform work created by the war. Air raid drills became a constant part of American life, and civilian air raid wardens were assigned to see that citizens complied with the rather strict blackout procedures that had been specified by government. Meetings and awareness lectures were also conducted by these dedicated people, who served on a volunteer basis.

Most police departments found it necessary to mobilize auxiliary police units to fill the vacancies created by the war. Auxiliary policemen were individuals who for one reason or another—advanced age, a physical infirmity, etc.—could not serve in the military. The auxiliary units were often activated by special legislation which stipulated that they would be disbanded when the war ended and the troops returned home. Auxiliary officers were generally full-time policemen, with limited police training, who acted as replacements for regular officers in the service. Auxiliary policemen performed admirably during their tours of duty and some gallantly forfeited their lives in defense of their communities. Some auxiliary police units, especially those in coastal cities where an enemy attack was considered a possibility, were trained in first aid, chemical warfare, and bomb dismantling procedures in case of invasion.

Reserve (part-time) police units were established in many communities. Reserve officers, who generally worked without pay, were put to work performing routine duties—traffic direction, guard duty, clerical work, etc. Reserve officers also rode with policemen to maintain two-man patrol cars.

Most major law enforcement agencies were subjected to basically the same war-related pressures; however, one department, the Metropolitan Police Department in the District of Columbia, found itself faced with a crisis, for all the obvious reasons. Although the exigencies that the men of the Metropolitan Police Department encountered were in many ways unique, their sacrifice and dedication in the face of adversity were typical of those made by their brothers nationwide.

With the declaration of war on December 7, 1941, the call upon the services of the Metropolitan Police Department increased rapidly. Some members of the department were immediately detailed to augment the White House police force, while others were dispatched to guard embassies, power plants, bridges, and other vital installations against sabotage. The Board of Commissioners afforded the department some relief when on March 5, 1942, it permitted the hiring of fifty special policemen, who were known as defense guards. These defense guards were strategically deployed so that policemen could be relieved for patrol duty. The department was fast losing its experienced manpower to the Armed Services. No fewer than 341 had either enlisted or been drafted. Civilian augmentation of the police department began, and six thousand volunteers were processed for an auxiliary police force. The Washington Police Academy was founded to train the recruits. Citizens from every walk of life generously offered their services as clerks, instructors, even laborers. Regular police personnel, after completing their tours of duty, often came back for another eight or ten hours of work with the volunteers. Precinct captains very often worked twenty-four hours a day, and dozens of volunteers worked in the precinct stations registering more auxiliary policemen. This grand force of Washington citizens, armed with a badge, an overseas cap, a raincoat, a web belt, whistle, baton, armband, and helmet, was a great deterrent to the commission of crime, not only during blackouts, but at other times. When the war ended, the *ad hoc* bodies of civilian volunteers disbanded after long and honorable service.[1]

## BLACK MARKETING

Although the rate of many classes of crimes fell during the war—in fact, the prison population even decreased for various reasons—certain war measures created added problems for the police. Every nation that has ever fought a war has had its share of citizens who made excessive profits from the sale of commodities in short supply. During earlier conflicts—the Civil War, the Spanish-American War, World War I—this activity was not generally unlawful; but with the coming of World War II drastic regulations were passed making war profiteering illegal. The Federal Government issued a list of fixed prices on selected commodities which made it unlawful to charge more than the stated price. In addition, there was rationing of certain goods. Some of the commodities affected by the war measures were meats, butter, and gasoline. The Office of Price Administration (OPA), the War Production Board, and the War Labor Board were created to regulate prices, to stabilize wages, and to regulate industrial allocation and proposal. In addition, there were hundreds of local ordinances which dealt with these issues. War profiteering occurred, though, and a term was popularized which referred to the illicit sale and purchase of commodities and goods—the black market.

The OPA organized the Enforcement Department which strenuously enforced black market ordinances. Between 1942 and 1947, there were 12,415 cases turned over to the United States

[1]Reprinted with editorial adaption from Howard V. Covell's "A Brief History of the Metropolitan Police Department," Washington: 1946, pp. 7-9.

Department of Justice for prosecution; all but 815, less than seven percent, were won by the government.[2]

The war measures also prompted other violations of the law as war profiteers stole and counterfeited ration currency, thus bringing the United States Secret Service and the FBI into cases. The competence and cunning of this new breed of counterfeiters presented an added challenge to Federal investigators who were forced to develop sophisticated new detection devices. Special lamps and chemical tests were but two of the techniques used to detect bogus or altered bills. Professional criminals, working freelance or with organized crime cartels, plagued the government and threatened the war effort.

Yet, despite fairly widespread violations of the war measures, the great mass of American citizens obeyed the law, displayed a remarkable tolerance for the rights of others, contributed to the war effort, and supported law enforcement, especially harried officers in municipal agencies.

## THE FBI AND INTERNAL SECURITY

When the situation in Europe had deteriorated to the point where it was obvious that American involvement in a war was imminent, President Franklin Delano Roosevelt moved to broaden the Federal Bureau of Investigation's internal security function. The President dispatched word to the FBI and to local police agencies of the Bureau's enlarged role:[3]

> The Attorney General has been requested by me to instruct the Federal Bureau of Investigation of the Department of Justice to take charge of investigative work in matters relating to espionage, sabotage, and violations of neutrality regulations. This task must be conducted in a comprehensive and effective manner on a national scale, and all information must be carefully sifted and correlated in order to avoid confusion and irresponsibility. To this end I request all police officers, sheriffs, and other law enforcement officers in the United States promptly to turn over to the nearest representative of the Federal Bureau of Investigation any information obtained by

[2]Marshal B. Clinard, *The Black Market* (Montclair, New Jersey: Patterson Smith Publishing Corp. Originally published in 1952, reprinted in 1969), p. 239.

[3]Harry and Bonaro Overstreet, *The FBI in Our Open Society* (New York: W. W. Norton and Company, Inc., 1969), pp. 88-89.

them relative to espionage, counterespionage, subversion activities, and violations of the neutrality laws.

The FBI opened field offices in Puerto Rico and the Canal Zone, and in six regions of the country where large military installations were located. The Army and Navy requested the Bureau to involve itself, in a limited way, in the security of defense plants producing war-related items. The Bureau created an intelligence division, along with a component for translating and decoding messages. The FBI's internal security work during the war was professionally carried out and amazingly successful. The image of the FBI as a superior investigative unit was once again enhanced— deservedly so.

## THE POSTWAR PERIOD

When the war ended, former policemen returned home to resume their careers in law enforcement. They were joined by other veterans, many of whom had been military policemen or special investigators, and a cadre of mature, well-trained, disciplined young men infused new blood into the police service. If this new breed of policemen had one shortcoming, it was that they were relatively uneducated, at least beyond high school. But there were no colleges on Iwo Jima, Guam, and Normandy, and furthermore, many institutions had discontinued their police programs for the duration of the war, making it unreasonable to demand advanced education from applicants. But the postwar period saw movement toward expanded educational programs for policemen, though it would be a decade before a significant number of police programs were created.

One of the most important postwar educational trends was the development of the junior college concept. While some sections of the country were slow to grasp the concept, one state— California—moved at breakneck speed in that direction, to the everlasting benefit of law enforcement. Police science seemed to fit perfectly into the junior college scheme of things. California also expanded its four-year programs, and police or criminology majors were created at Fresno State College, Los Angeles State College, and Sacramento State College. By the end of the decade Los Angeles had law enforcement programs at four institutions of higher learning—a junior college, a state college, a state university, and a private university. The Los Angeles Police Department, about which more will be said in the following chapter, was destined to ascend to a status of leadership in many areas of police work, thanks in no small measure to the educational attainments of its personnel, 3,000 of whom were hired between 1945 and 1950. It is no coincidence that those police departments which had within commuting range specialized educational programs, and who encouraged their officers to enroll in college, rose to a position of respect in their field (e.g. Berkeley, Wichita, Los Angeles).

The postwar period saw a good deal of progress in the area of police training. Recruit and in-service training programs burgeoned as municipal law enforcement agencies converted their hastily established wartime schools for auxiliary officers into full-fledged police academies. The period 1946-1949 was termed by one police scholar as "the period of greatest activity" in the police training field.[4] In 1948 the Los Angeles Police Department became the first police agency in the country to inaugurate a system of roll call training, whereby uniformed officers were given brief periods of intensified training immediately prior to going on duty. By the end of the decade most every department of any size had a police academy. Those that did not usually sent their recruits to nearby training schools or engaged in on-the-job training. The South, which had lagged sadly behind the rest of the nation in establishing police training courses, began to catch up as New Orleans, Miami, and Augusta inaugurated training schools.

The decade also saw a movement toward adopting some of the technological achievements of an increasingly mobile society. For example, in 1948 the New York Police Department became the first major agency to employ a police helicopter for patrol purposes.

## CONCLUSION

Returning World War II veterans, toughened and matured by military service, provided police departments with a source of manpower of unquestioned value. Young, dynamic, dedicated to police work, these youthful veterans were badly needed by law enforcement agencies, which for a half decade had marked time as

---

[4]Allen Z. Gammage, *Police Training in the United States* (Springfield, Illinois: Charles C Thomas, Publisher, 1963), p. 21.

far as progress was concerned. The postwar period saw some movement toward professionalization, but it was mostly a time in which many departments searched for positive direction. The sudden influx of personnel into previously poorly staffed agencies created the need for updated training programs and the nation's police departments were kept busy just selecting, processing, training, and breaking-in recruits. For the second time in two decades the FBI successfully stepped into a breach produced by an explosive social phenomenon. The FBI had earned the respect of a greatful nation. In many ways the FBI provided local law enforcement with direction, for the Bureau had dramatically illustrated what a police component could do if it was staffed by competent, well-educated personnel who were provided with advanced training and the most modern hardware, and who were allowed to ply their trade relatively free from the influence of politicians.

William H. Parker, Chief of Police, City of Los Angeles. *(Official photograph of the Los Angeles Police Department)*

*Chapter 10*

# THE EMERGENCE OF THE CALIFORNIA POLICE (1950–1959)

## THE KEFAUVER COMMITTEE'S INQUIRY

The new decade had hardly begun when a police scandal of major proportions was exposed, a scandal that shook the very foundation of the urban system of law enforcement. In 1950 an accumulation of facts motivated governmental action to investigate crime in interstate commerce. On May 10, the Senate Crime Committee was born, chaired by Senator Estes Kefauver of Tennessee. What the committee found was a web of graft, corruption, and organized crime.

The Kefauver Committee, as it became known, conducted a national investigation into organized crime. Committee members New York City, Chicago, Cleveland, Miami, Tampa, Kansas, St. Louis, Detroit, Philadelphia, and Las Vegas where they found that:[1]

> A nationwide crime syndicate does exist in the United States of America, despite the protestations of a strangely assorted company of criminals, self-serving politicians, plain blind fools, and others who may be honestly misguided that there is no such combine.

Witnesses by the hundreds were summoned to testify before the committee and the names of crime cartel members became household words—Joe Adonis, Frank Costello, Anthony Accardo, "Lucky" Luciano. The syndicate was found to be run by an international criminal organization called the Mafia. Nearly everywhere the committee went, it found constables, police officers, and detectives who took bribes to protect gamblers and prostitutes from prosecution. Bigger fry—sheriffs, police chiefs, and command officers—were found to be on the syndicate's payroll, too. A police captain in Chicago admitted to receiving a

---

[1] Estes Kefauver, *Crime In America* (New York: Greenwood Press, Publishers, 1968), p. 12.

$30,000 "gift" from a gambler. The Sheriff of Dade County, Florida, acknowledged that his assets had grown from $2,500 to $70,000 during his five years in office, all on a $7,500 a year salary. In addition, his wife had transported more than $25,000 out of state, presumably for safekeeping. In Tampa the Sheriff of Hillsborough County was indicted by a grand jury for taking protection money from a gambler and for neglect of duty. In Kansas City, syndicate members were shown to have a hand in police department promotions. The police commissioner of East St. Louis, Missouri, an elected public official, was found to have collected $131,425 in "political contributions" in six years on which he dutifully paid income taxes, and banked. It was discovered that the day John J. Grosch was elected to the office of criminal sheriff of Orleans Parish (New Orleans), he was given a new Cadillac limousine by "unnamed friends." Other sheriffs in Louisiana refused to answer crime commission queries about why they banked more money per year than their yearly salary. The story was the same in Detroit, New York, Las Vegas, Philadelphia, and elsewhere.

Exposures of crime and corruption had occured before in America with only minor public outrage, but this time things were different, thanks to the youthful television industry. The committee's hearings were televised to the nation, and the myth of the sinister, cunning, shrewd criminal that had been foisted on the public by books and in films, was exploded as the flesh-and-blood criminal was exposed to be a bumbling, rather oafish individual whose command of the English language left something to be desired. Millions of viewers watched enthralled as an almost endless parade of hoodlums immortalized the phrase: "I refuse to testify on the grounds that it might tend to incriminate me."

The Kefauver proceedings had a significant impact on the American people in two respects: (1) they shattered the traditional image of the sinewy, brainy criminal, and (2) they showed how easy it was to corrupt the nation's underpaid police forces. By 1951 wholesale police reforms were being undertaken by urban communities which had suffered a televised black eye. Some reformers harkened back two decades to the reports of the Wickersham Commission as they sought to upgrade their departments. The type of corruption uncovered by both Wickersham and Kefauver had come from the top of governmental pyramids and had infected the entire structure. One answer to this problem was not simple but it was basic—end corrupt political domination of police departments. Police chief appointment procedures were updated, the operating relationship between police executives and higher authority was revised, and more independence was given to police commanders by elected public officials, who began to stand somewhat aloof from their police departments for fear of charges of tampering.

Even though corruption was widespread, not all communities that were visited by the Kefauver Committee were found to have corrupt police forces. Quite the contrary, a number of very fine police agencies actually received enthusiastic commendations from the senator from Tennessee. One of Senator Kefauver's most glowing testimonials was directed at an agency which he described as a "white spot" in the nation's pattern of crime—the Los Angeles Police Department. Led by Los Angeles, the entire state of California was to be thrust into supremacy in the police field within the short space of a decade.

## THE CALIFORNIA POLICE

California had had bright spots in policing since the turn of the century. For example, the Berkeley Police Department under August Vollmer had been well thought of nationally for years, as had other departments of similar size. But, although Berkeley could offer a model for professional law enforcement, its very size prevented it from having a dramatic impact on policing in the state. It did not dominate a region because it was not a core city. But Los Angeles was a core city and when the Los Angeles police initiated serious reform, a trend was begun which rapidly spread to all areas of the state. Soon the LAPD became a world famous police organization.

One of the most significant actions in the history of American law enforcement occurred on August 9, 1950, when William H. Parker was appointed Chief of Police of the City of Los Angeles. Parker had been in the police service since 1927, working his way through the ranks to chief. During the Depression, and while still employed by the police department, he received an LL.B degree from the Los Angeles College of Law. When the Depression ended and a mass exodus of college-educated men from police ranks occurred, Parker chose to remain in the police service. Chief Parker served his country during World War II, receiving a Purple Heart for wounds received during the Normandy Invasion, along with the French Croix de Guerre with Silver Star, and the Italian Star of Solidarity.

Chief Parker recognized the absolute necessity of employing only superior personnel. He toughened up entry level procedures, and it showed. Six months after his appointment, the Los Angeles Police Department probably had the most stringent selection procedures in the country. During one patrolman's examination only 17 of 2,300 applicants passed the written examination.

Much has been said of William H. Parker, but perhaps the most accurate commentary was made by another great police administrator, O. W. Wilson:[2]

> I have watched his operations and the progress of his department with an interest stimulated by the discovery that he was making the most of his rare opportunity to modernize and professionalize police service. He immediately reorganized his department to simplify and assure his control over its operations and to facilitate the attainment of police objectives. He also adopted the best of known police procedures and urged his exceptionally qualified staff to develop new ones. . . .What Parker was doing required more courage than is possessed by most men. . . .

Not only did the Los Angeles Police Department serve as a model of what a law enforcement agency should be, but William H. Parker offered a shining example of the "new breed" American police administrator. Some of Parker's operational innovations included:

1. Formation of an internal affairs division to investigate citizen complaints of police misconduct.
2. Co-authorship of a city Board of Rights procedure guaranteeing the separation of police discipline from politics.
3. Creation of a bureau of administration, which included two new components: the intelligence and the planning and research divisions.
4. Establishment of an intensive community relations program.
5. The disbursement of a fleet of patrol helicopters.
6. Enactment of a strict firearms use policy that included

---

[2]O. W. Wilson, *Parker on Police* (Springfield: Charles C Thomas, Publisher, 1957), p. vii.

internal department review of all weapons discharges.
7. The construction of a modern police administration building. Five million dollars in savings was realized because of Chief Parker's planning.

California experienced an economic boom during the 1950s as industry, business, and commerce attracted millions of new residents to the state. A virtual technological revolution occurred. The aircraft industry centered its activities in California, along with countless electronics concerns, communications companies, and shipping interests. Salaries for workers were raised in order to attract professional talent from out of state. California constructed a massive freeway system to handle its burgeoning auto traffic. Institutions of higher learning, especially junior colleges, were opened at an unprecedented rate, and they were tuition free. The phenomenal growth caused both problems and opportunities for the California police.

In the field of higher education, some three score public institutions were opened by the end of the decade. The increased demands for police services, coupled with higher salaries and the growing complexity of the police task, led to the creation of law enforcement programs at many of these colleges. By the end of the decade, there were forty-three separate institutions which awarded degrees in law enforcement or a related subject. Thirty-five were junior colleges. Over seventy-six percent of the nation's two-year law enforcement programs were in California. Motivated by the easy access to a free quality education, California's policemen flocked to enroll in school. In 1958 Allen P. Bristow wrote that "Peace officers throughout the state are utilizing these educational opportunities to a great degree."[3] Within a decade the police in California had raised their educational level significantly and, as a whole, became the country's best educated group of municipal officers.

In the area of training, California again led the way as departments established and expanded pre-service and in-service training programs, a number of which became affiliated with the state's junior colleges. The California Highway Patrol symbolized the

[3]Allen P. Bristow, "Junior Colleges Play Important Role in Professionalization," *California Peace Officer* (Sacramento: Peace Officer's Assoc. of State of Calif., July-Aug., 1958), p. 35.

state's emphasis in this area when in 1954 it constructed a massive training academy on 224 acres of ground in Sacramento for the initial cost of $625,000. In 1959 the State of California created by legislative action the Peace Officers' Standards and Training (POST) Commission to require statewide standards for recruiting and training personnel.

At a time when other states were experiencing difficulties with corrupt elected sheriffs, California's system of county law enforcement showed remarkable stability. In many ways the stable sheriff system was typified by the Los Angeles County Sheriff's Department, a superior agency. When Sheriff Peter J. Pitchess, a former FBI agent with a law degree, was elected in 1958, he was only the second man to hold that office since 1932. Under Sheriff Pitchess' administration technological and administrative innovations were adopted and the police academy was expanded in size and in scope until it had attained a worldwide reputation for creative programs.

The story was the same in almost all sections of the state: a highly trained, well-educated, and higher-paid class of policemen that made good use of advanced technology and management techniques. It was not difficult to figure out why the police in California had made such remarkable progress. The public and government had committed themselves to the idea of honest, efficient, and professional law enforcement, free from the domineering influence of corrupt politicians.

## DEVELOPMENTS IN MUNICIPAL POLICING

To allege that the only bright spot on the national law enforcement scene in the 1950s was California is to perpetrate a fraud. Admittedly, California was the first state to professionalize their police on so grand a scale—and on such a statewide level—but some states and communities were moving in that direction, and a number of police agencies in other parts of the country were striving to professionalize at breakneck speed.

Negro civil rights actions surfaced in the 1950s, led by the National Association for the Advancement of Colored People (NAACP). Most movement in that direction was conducted in court, though some strategies involved open demonstrations. Those few unlawful demonstrations that did occur were nonviolent in nature. As a result some police administrators began to

A Philadelphia Police Department "motor bandit patrol car" taking a call from headquarters as it patrols its assigned area, usually a part of the city where the incidence of crime was highest. *(Courtesy of the Philadelphia Police Department)*

view their responsibilities as more than just the protection of life and property and preservation of the peace. A few forward thinking executives foresaw racial problems approaching, and they moved to improve relations between their departments and the community. In 1957 the St. Louis Police Department created the nation's first formal police-community-relations component. But law enforcement was slow to act in this area, for it was an era in which the management principles of business and industry had been adopted by chiefs of police desirous of upgrading their function, and to reassign manpower from street duty to community-relations work was considered wasteful by many police commanders. That outlook was to change drastically during the next decade.

Specialized police training programs were expanded during the decade. In 1951 Michigan State University initiated a four-week basic police course, along with a one-week command school. That same year the Southern Police Institute was established and twelve-week training courses were offered to supervisory, administrative, and command officers. The Institute was housed on the campus of the University of Louisville. In 1953 the Police Training Institute of the University of Illinois was operationalized to train the state's police officers, especially recruit officers. In 1959 the New York State legislature enacted the New York Municipal Police Training Act, making it the first state to mandate minimum training requirements for municipal policemen.

In 1950 two books were published that had a remarkable, although not immediate, effect on municipal policing: O. W. Wilson's *Police Administration* and *Municipal Police Administration,* 3rd edition, by the International City Managers' Association. Police executives nationwide utilized the principles contained in the two works to reform their agencies. Both books became giants in the field, but Wilson's remains a classic. By the middle of the decade the nation's superior police departments, now for the first time in history more than a handful, reflected the basic but innovative tenets set down by Wilson, who had battle-tested his philosophy in the field. The writings of O. W. Wilson and the ICMA have had a profound effect on the American police service.

## CONCLUSION

There were a number of bright lights in law enforcement by the end of the decade and, although most of them were in California, other sections of the country were also beginning to move forward. Admittedly, though, the struggle to professionalize was a fragmented effort rather than a nationwide march. Municipal law enforcement was making considerable progress toward freeing itself from the clutches of partisan political influence, a major step toward honest, efficient policing. Things were indeed progressing well, albeit at a slower clip than many professionals liked. But storm clouds were on the horizon; and the police, as they had so many other times in their history, were about to face a trying time.

## Chapter 11

# PROTEST, POLITICS, AND THE STRUGGLE TO PROFESSIONALIZE (1960-1969)

$T$he 1960s comprised a decade in which the concept of police professionalism progressed from a regional commitment to a national movement. It was also a decade in which the police, especially municipal officers, found themselves under fire—verbally, physically, and philosophically—from critics of everything from an unpopular war to the welfare system.

During the era citizens with grievances ignored traditional avenues of redress and took to the streets to protest. Negro civil rights demonstrations escalated, but angry and impatient minority group members also engaged in tumultuous riots and civil disturbances. Student unrest exploded into reality as college students, protesting the war in Vietnam and American social conditions, engaged in violent and disruptive campus protests which often spilled over into city streets. The crime rate escalated. Narcotics addiction threatened to reach epidemic proportions. Extremist groups at both ends of the political spectrum were organized. Political assassinations occurred with depressing regularity. And in the middle, as government's most visible representatives, were the police, trying desperately to maintain some semblence of order in the face of unrestrained political passions, attempting to assume a professional stance against some of the deadliest and most provocative tactics ever used by protestors. All the while the crime rate rose astronomically.

## THE CRIME PROBLEM

From 1960-1969 the population of the country rose approximately thirteen percent, while reported crimes rose 148 percent. Some of the increase could be attributed to better methods of crime reporting; however, it was clear that crime—serious crime—was increasing at an alarming rate: aggravated assault rose 102 percent; forcible rape was up 116 percent; robbery climbed 177

135

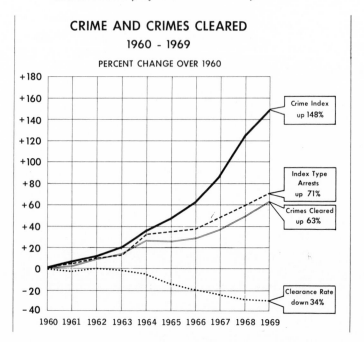

(Courtesy of the FBI's *Uniform Crime Reports*)

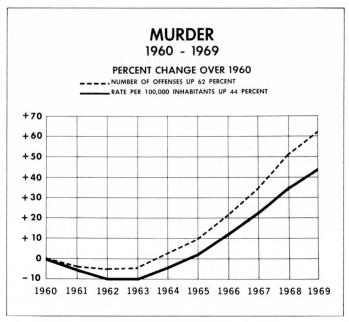

(Courtesy of the FBI's *Uniform Crime Reports*)

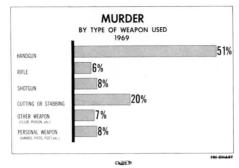

(Courtesy of the FBI's *Uniform Crime Reports*)

percent; burglary rose 117 percent, and murder went up 62 percent.[1] In addition to an upsurge in traditional crimes, other types of crimes rose significantly, and although the movement to professionalize the police was beginning to show measureable results, the decade began, as had the previous one, with a disturbing exposé of police lawlessness.

### Police Corruption

In January, 1960, eight Chicago policemen were arrested for complicity in a professional burglary ring when a professional burglar with whom they had been working informed on them. The police had allowed him to ply his trade for a cut of the profits. It took four police vans to haul the contraband from the officers' homes.[2]

Citizens of Denver were stunned when later that year thirty members of their police department were key principals in a half-million-dollar burglary ring. The "Police Burglars of Denver" was front page news nationwide.[3]

Also in 1960 the New York State Investigation Commission uncovered a collusive relationship between policemen in Buffalo and vice lords. Gambling and prostitution were allowed to flourish

---

[1] Federal Bureau of Investigation, *Uniform Crime Reports—1969* (Washington: U. S. Government Printing Office, 1970).

[2] Ralph Lee Smith, *The Tarnished Badge* (New York: Thomas Y. Crowell Company, 1965), pp. 157-173.

[3] *Ibid.*, pp. 14-40.

while officers looked the other way and actually issued courtesy cards to racketeers, granting them membership in honorary police societies.[4]

The following year a CBS television documentary entitled "Biography of a Bookie Joint" showed Boston policemen entering and leaving with great frequency a South Boston Horse Parlor. In later public hearings, the Police Commissioner resigned.[5]

In January, 1964, twenty-three gambling-related indictments were handed down by a Marion County, Indiana, grand jury. Twenty-two of the indictments were for Indianapolis police officers, only three of whom were patrolmen.[6]

The frequency of the corruption together with the apparent widespread nature of it—the exposés pointed to a national malady rather than regional problem—once again motivated police reform. Probably the most significant upheaval occurred in Chicago, where O. W. Wilson was appointed Superintendant of Police. Significant innovations were initiated by the legendary police administrator and within a relatively brief period of time public confidence was restored in the beleaguered Chicago Police Department.

## Political Assassinations

Political passions reached such fever pitch in the 1960s that the most direct and dreaded form of protest—murder—was invoked on a shocking number of occasions. Politicians, civil rights leaders, and controversial heads of extremist groups were gunned down by men whose motivation and mental stability differed in almost every case. And the incidents of political assassination were not sectional occurrences; apparently no part of the nation was immune from them. As usual, local police officials, occasionally assisted by Federal Officers, were assigned the task of investigating each offense and bringing the assailant to justice. The assassinations placed extreme pressures on the police agencies in whose jurisdiction they were perpetrated. Most handled their responsibilities

[4]*Ibid.*

[5]William J. Bopp, *The Police Rebellion* (Springfield: Charles C Thomas, Publisher, 1971) p. 173.

[6]*Supra* note 2, pp. 122-147.

in a competent and professional manner. Some, however, were not equal to the task.

In 1962 in Jackson, Mississippi, Medgar Evers, field representative of the NAACP, was gunned down in front of his home. He died a short time later. Local and state police, together with agents from the FBI, worked on the case until a white segregationist was arrested and brought to trial.

The following year President John F. Kennedy was shot and killed from ambush as he rode in a Dallas, Texas, motorcade. Several hours later the suspected assailant was captured, but not before he had killed Dallas police officer J.D. Tippet. The President's alleged assassin was also killed when he was shot in the basement garage of the police station by an enraged Dallas nightclub operator who had gained access to the scene.

Later in the decade two extremist leaders—one black and one white—were shot and killed by former followers. Malcolm X, previously a Black Muslim and leader of the Nationalistic Organization for Afro-American Unity, was felled by a hail of bullets as he addressed a group of four hundred blacks in New York City's Audubon Ballroom. George Lincoln Rockwell, founder and head of the American Nazi Party, was killed by gunfire in the parking lot of an Arlington, Virginia, shopping center. In both cases the police arrested and brought the killers to justice.

The assassinations of the Reverend Martin Luther King, Jr., in Memphis, and Senator Robert F. Kennedy in Los Angeles, stunned the nation. Their killers were arrested, brought to trial, and convicted through the use of tried and true police investigative techniques.

### Mass Murders

Although no civilized society can excuse or condone political murders, most were committed by a man or men with a purpose, albeit a grisly one. One type of deadly crime during the decade was so irrational, so purposeless that the sanity of the perpetrators had to be questioned, and usually was in later court trials. The number of senseless mass murders during the decade, together with the inflammatory publicity surrounding them, terrorized communities across the land.

In Chicago Richard Speck murdered eight student nurses in their quarters. In Boston, the "Boston Strangler" plied his deadly trade as that city and the nation watched in horror. In Los Angeles, Charles Manson's "family" had its name indelibly etched on the blackest pages of American history. But "the crime of the century" occurred in Austin, Texas, on the campus of the University of Texas, on a hot afternoon in August, 1966, when Charles Whitman secreted himself in a tower 307 feet above the sprawling campus and, with a veritable arsenal of weapons at his side, shot forty-four people, thirteen fatally. Three policemen and a civilian ascended the tower where Whitman was encountered and shot to death. Although a later investigation and autopsy revealed that Whitman was suffering from a brain tumor and had been consuming Dexedrine tablets, neither the tumor nor the stimulants were believed responsible for his actions. The ultimate explanation of the conduct of the "mad man in the tower" died with Whitman.

### A FUSILLADE FROM THE SUPREME COURT

During a time when police officers were waging a frontal attack on crime and violence, the United States Supreme Court, led by Chief Justice Earl Warren, released a number of court decisions that were highly critical of police action.

In *Mapp v. Ohio* (1961) the court held that the Fourth Amendment of the Constitution applies to all the states through the due process clause of the Fourteenth Amendment. In *Gideon v. Wainright* (1963) the court required that states must appoint counsel for indigent defendants in both capital and noncapital cases. The court decided in *Escobedo v. Illinois* (1964) that when the police process shifts from the investigatory to the accusatory stage, and its purpose is to elicit a confession, the subject must be allowed to consult with an attorney. In *Miranda v. Arizona* (1966) the Supreme Court held that policemen must advise suspects of certain Constitutional guarantees in order to make a confession admissible as evidence. In addition the court stated that the privilege against self-incrimination applied to police interrogations as well as to court hearings. Two later cases related to the American juvenile court system. In *Kent v. United States* (1966) the Warren Court held that a juvenile court must grant defendants a hearing prior to transferring jurisdiction to a criminal court, while in re Gault (1967) it was decided that the due process clause of the Fourteenth Amendment was applicable to state juvenile courts. It is interesting to note that of these six major landmark decisions, four were decided by a five to four vote.

As a result of these Supreme Court decisions, a clamor arose against the Warren Court, not only from within police ranks but also from the general public, though a move to impeach the Chief Justice drew little backing. Policemen became disturbed over the rulings, partly because they restricted police power and authority during time of crisis, but mostly because the police felt they were thrust into the position of having to anticipate Supreme Court action. Police actions in many of the earlier landmark cases had been considered legal and prudent by lower courts and appellate tribunals; however, the Warren Court, often by a five to four vote, negated earlier precedents and lower court rulings. What was perfectly legal one year was often ruled illegal retroactively a year or two later by the Supreme Court. Opinion polls showed that a majority of the American public felt that the "pendulum had swung too far to the left," and that court was "coddling criminals."

## MILITANCY AND THE POLICE

The social atmosphere of the 1960s was strikingly similar to that which existed during earlier eras. Militancy, protest, civil unrest, and the rise of extremist groups appeared in great, and intermingled, profusion. Again, like the turmoil of a bygone period, the police were assigned to combat disorders and, in so doing, contracted a case of militancy themselves.

### Racial Protest and Urban Rioting

The nonviolent Negro protest that had originated in the previous decade escalated in the sixties as moderate black leaders were able to enlist broad support for their cause. Massive demonstrations filled city streets, and in the majority of cases, demonstrations were remarkably free of violence, due in no small measure to good police handling, a talent that was learned more by field experience and sound administrative leadership than through tactical training programs. Besides massive demonstrations and lengthy protest marches, other tactics were undertaken. Sit-ins, wade-ins, voter registration drives, boycotts, and rent strikes were only a few of the devices employed by protestors. And although the police were only occasionally the targets of protest, demonstrators found that an "incident" involving local law enforcement officers could serve to more dramatically publicize their demands. In fact, Stokely Charmichael, an early leader of the Student Non-Violent Coordinating Committee (SNCC), stated that a demonstration which did not provoke a police response was unsuccessful. On a number of occasions demonstrations did provoke extreme police action, and the entire law enforcement community suffered because of the ill-advised actions of a few departments.

By mid-decade the cry for desegregation had been smothered by urban black rioting, striking first in the Watts section of Los Angeles, but spreading quickly to other cities—Tampa, Cincinnati, Atlanta, Newark, Detroit, Miami, and Chicago to mention but a few. The police, ill-trained, badly equipped, and unprepared for such disorders, were thrown into the breach. Criticized by conservatives for being too permissive, accused by liberals of overreacting, law enforcement officers tried to restore order to communities that often simultaneously made conflicting demands on them. Policemen came under attack from all quarters for their handling of racial rioting. By 1966 a new philosophy had pervaded the civil rights movement as "we shall overcome" was replaced by "black power" and "burn, baby, burn." An additional threat to the police surfaced with the rise of black nationalist groups, such as the Black Panther Party (BPP), the Republic of New Africa, the United Slaves (US), who believed in such direct action as murder and arson. Policemen became targets for snipers as black reactionaries stockpiled weapons and used them to shoot down officers

*Police Killed by Felons, 1960–1969*

| Type of Police activity | Total | Type of assignment | | | | | |
|---|---|---|---|---|---|---|---|
| | | 2-man cars | 1-man cars | | Foot | Detective and special assignment | Off duty |
| | | | Alone | Assisted | | | |
| Total | 561 | 164 | *153 | 53 | 34 | 111 | 46 |
| 1. Responding to "disturbance" calls (family quarrels, man with gun, etc.) | 107 | 47 | 17 | 14 | 9 | 16 | 4 |
| 2. Burglaries in progress or pursuing burglary suspects | 53 | 16 | 21 | 3 | 1 | 11 | 1 |
| 3. Robberies in progress or pursuing robbery suspects | 112 | 26 | 26 | 13 | 7 | 21 | 19 |
| 4. Attempting other arrests | 157 | 39 | 49 | 15 | 9 | 33 | 12 |
| 5. Handling, transporting, custody of prisoners | 36 | 11 | 10 | 1 | ---------- | 13 | 1 |
| 6. Investigating suspicious persons and circumstances | 53 | 13 | 26 | 1 | 3 | 8 | 2 |
| 7. Ambush, deranged persons (no warning-unprovoked attack) | 43 | 12 | 4 | 6 | 5 | 9 | 7 |

*99 city police officers, 54 county and State police officers.

(Courtesy of the FBI's *Uniform Crime Reports*)

**Police Killed by Felons, 1960–1969**

| Type of Police activity | Total | Region | | | |
|---|---|---|---|---|---|
| | | North-eastern States | North Central States | Southern States | Western States |
| 1. Responding to "disturbance" calls (family quarrels, man with gun, etc.) | 107 | 20 | 32 | 39 | 16 |
| 2. Burglaries in progress or pursuing burglary suspects | 53 | 4 | 15 | 20 | 14 |
| 3. Robberies in progress or pursuing robbery suspects | 112 | 25 | 34 | 31 | 22 |
| 4. Attempting other arrests | 157 | 17 | 27 | 90 | 23 |
| 5. Handling, transporting, custody of prisoners | 36 | 4 | 9 | 21 | 2 |
| 6. Investigating suspicious persons and circumstances | 53 | 5 | 13 | 21 | 14 |
| 7. Ambush, deranged persons (no warning—unprovoked attack) | 43 | 9 | 13 | 14 | 7 |
| Total | 561 | 84 | 143 | 236 | 98 |

(Courtesy of the FBI's *Uniform Crime Reports*)

from ambush. Confrontations between policemen and Black Panthers consistently led to bloody consequences, which more often than not brought cries of police harassment from Panthers. At one point the police were accused of "murdering" twenty-nine Panthers, and news services, magazines, newspapers, and television networks accepted the number and the accusation as true, even though the source was a BPP attorney. After the claim had been made, accepted, and published or broadcast, the *New Yorker* magazine, in a brilliantly incisive job of investigative reporting, exposed the claim and the figure as contrived and false.

## Student Unrest

In 1964 student unrest exploded into reality when a sit-in demonstration at the University of California at Berkeley turned into the largest case of mass civil disobedience in California's history as 830 police officers from a variety of agencies arrested 773 persons. Motivated by a number of causes but rallying around a common belief in the invalidity of the Vietnam War, student protest spread like wildfire from campus to campus. Names like Kent State, Columbia, Berkeley, and Jackson State became household words as peaceful protest evolved into massive acts of civil disobedience, then into riotous activity. Marches on draft boards were conducted, often deteriorating to extreme collective violence, amidst the now familiar cries of "police brutality." Radical students, many of whom were from affluent backgrounds, formed associations, such as the Students for a Democratic Society (SDS), the Progressive Labor Party (PLP), the Socialist Workers Party (SWP), or the Venceremos Brigade (VB). Although the ideology and political orientation differed among the various

Police brutality? A participant in a "peace" demonstration in Oakland, California, is about to strike a police officer from behind with a pipe concealed in a sheet of rolled newspaper.

The age of militancy. College students "doing their thing." *(Courtesy of the St. Petersburg Police Department)*

organizations, their goal was the same: smash the American "system." Failing to receive widespread support, some groups and individuals went underground and engaged in isolated terroristic tactics. Explosions rocked a number of governmental buildings, and several innocent people were killed through indiscriminate acts of wanton terrorism. Violent student unrest reached its peak in 1968, when during the Democratic National Convention in Chicago, thousands of angry demonstrators clashed with police, thus bringing denunciations of the student protest movement by conservatives and bitter accusations of abusive and excessive police action by liberals. As a result of the incident, the split between liberals and the police, always present to some extent, became a chasm. Student lawlessness tended to muddy the traditional police view of criminality, for here were large groups of affluent, college-educated young people engaging in violent, disruptive acts and felonious conduct, a situation with which policemen were unfamiliar. Gone now was that rather clear-cut police image of the criminal which saw law violators as coming from economically deprived, uneducated, lower-class groupings.

## The Cities' Response To Violence: Police Review Boards

American's cities, faced with growing internal strife, sought to alleviate some of the causative factors of civil insurrection by establishing extraordinary community relations programs. Many communities created imaginative programs of substance and merit, but others chose to implement superficial, stopgap devices aimed more at pacifying minority group leadership than attacking the underlying causes of their frustrations. One such device was the police review board.

The concept of the police review board, a panel of citizens established to hear public grievances against individual officers, was not new; the idea dated back to the 1930s, and the city of Philadelphia even established one in 1958. But it was not until the 1960s that the idea was operationalized to any great extent.

Proponents of review boards viewed the clashes between blacks and policemen as a deep-seated problem which had to be corrected immediately. Abrasive police-Negro relationships were not, in fact, the most pressing problem; they were a symptom of a greater dilemma, for the police as governments' most visible repre-sentatives simply manned the barricades against citizens with complaints against higher authority. For city fathers to send their officers out to hold back a demonstration of jobless men, then after the two groups had clashed to suggest that what was needed was a police review board to attack the problem was, at best, shallow thinking. Yet that is basically what happened. City officials in community after community established police review boards, thereby attacking a symptom of a multifaceted problem which went unsolved.

Police review boards had basic structural and philosophical weaknesses which doomed them to failure from the start. First, they were discriminatory. Of all the components of city government, only the police were forced to labor directly under citizen scrutiny, a situation which did not go unnoticed in the law enforcement community. Second, citizens served on boards without pay and with no special training. The result was a high personnel-turnover rate that contributed to a lack of continuity in the decision-making process. Third, the lack of sophistication of board members led to fewer sustained complaints against policemen than in the earlier systems of internal police review, giving the impression that police review panels were overly lenient, thereby alienating the people who were supposed to benefit most from the plan. Fourth, review boards, although advisory in nature, wrested from chiefs of police the responsibility for meting out internal discipline, an unhealthy situation at best. Fifth, the boards' procedures often refused to grant policemen the most basic protections of due process. Last, implementors of the review board concept failed to anticipate the depth and intensity of police resistance to it. Although the boards were attacked primarily for their administrative weaknesses, there is evidence which indicates that review boards were more a symbolic issue to police officers, who saw them as a liberal capitulation in the face of urban violence.

Police review boards were established in Rochester; York, Pennsylvania; Minneapolis, and New York City. In each city they were bitterly opposed by rank-and-file patrolmen's associations who, through referenda, lobbying, and court action, succeeded in eliminating the device from their communities. The fight over civilian review in New York City began as a typical labor-management dispute; but before it was over, it had evolved into one of the most significant events in police history, an incident which ranks in importance with the Boston Police Strike of 1919.

In 1966 Mayor John Lindsay added four civilians to the New York Police Department's Complaint Review Board, which had been manned previously by three deputy police commissioners. The move was resisted by the 25,000-member Patrolmen's Benevolent Association (PBA), which sought to force a referendum on the issue. Strangely, the PBA's plan to have the citizens of New York City vote on the idea was strenuously opposed by Mayor Lindsay, a civil libertarian, who battled, unsuccessfully, to keep the measure off the ballot. Against tremendous odds and with the state's three most influential political figures—Lindsay, Senator Jacob Javits, and Senator Robert F. Kennedy—on the other side, the "Lindsay plan" went to the electorate, which voted it out of existence by an astounding 1,313,161 to 765,468. Never in history had patrolmen waged so brazen a battle against their bosses and won.[7]

The significance of the NYPBA's victory went far beyond the city limits of New York. Patrolmen across the nation learned from the PBA's experience that they possessed political muscle which, once flexed, could bring substantial rewards. A movement toward police militancy was started in New York City, a movement that shows no sign of abating.

### Police Militancy

Policemen, particularly patrolmen in urban areas, sick of unfavorable court decisions, battle-weary from policing demonstrations and riots, tired of extreme liberal criticism, but buoyed by the success of the New York Patrolmen's Benevolent Association, set out to better their economic lot by utilizing old-fashioned, not so subtle, trade union tactics. Police associations and fraternal organizations which had originally been founded for social and benevolent purposes were transformed into professional confederations whose new concern was with bread-and-butter issues. Membership in the Fraternal Order of Police (FOP) burgeoned to over 100,000. Fragmented local police organizations banded together in state and national consortia for lobbying purposes. A national police union was created, although early recruitment was spotty.

[7]*Supra* note 5, pp. 10, 133.

Almost from the occurrence of the historic event in New York City, a series of labor-management disputes developed that were settled only after extreme measures had been taken by patrolmen. In November, 1966, patrolmen in Pontiac, Michigan, called in sick, en masse, to enforce demands for a wage increase. This tactic, termed the "blue flu," was to become widespread. During the spring of 1967 patrolmen in Detroit engaged in a ticket slow-

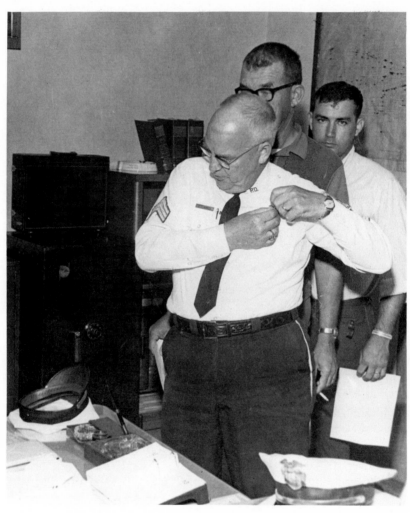

Police militancy. Members of the Plant City, Florida, Police Department line up to turn in their badges after a dispute with city officials over a pay increase.

down and sick-strike in quest of a pay raise. On July 17, 1969, the first strike of uniformed employees in the history of the State of California occurred when the Vallejo police and fire departments walked off their jobs for five days. "Job actions"—work slow-downs and stoppages; strikes; ticket blizzards (the writing of large numbers of nonrevenue-producing traffic citations), mass resignations—occurred in literally hundreds of communities, large and small, including Boston; New York; Minneapolis; Atlanta; San Diego; Plant City, Florida; Chicago Heights, Illinois; and Poplar Bluff, Missouri. Policemen began receiving generous pay increases and fringe benefits, but they were paying a heavy price for it in public support, even though the overwhelming number of police officers in the country never engaged in extreme acts. Many policemen viewed with ambivalence the actions of rebellious officers. It was obvious that trade-unionist principles were not compatible with the idea of police professionalization but it was hard to argue with success, especially when success manifested itself in such tangible ways.

## Empirical Inquiry into Crime, Riots, and Police Activity

The social conditions of the decade—termed by iconoclasts the "sick sixties"—spurred official governmental inquiries into the problems of the era. Commissions were appointed, grand juries convened, committees formed, and task forces flooded communities to uncover the causes and preventions of various social dilemmas. Many of the commissions were *ad hoc* bodies assigned to investigate specific incidents: a riot, student unrest at a college, a lawful demonstration that had deteriorated into a tumultuous assembly, or questionable police tactics in restoring civil order. Other commissions, especially those appointed by the President of the United States, were formed to probe a general social problem: crime, civil disorder, violence, etc.

Unfortunately, by the time most commissions released their investigative results to the public, opinion on the issues in question had polarized and the findings generally pleased only those whose previously held views were reinforced. In fact, commissions, especially Presidential commissions, became an issue themselves as more often than not they recommended grandiose solutions with a price tag which the public and politicians refused to accept. In addition to official inquiries, individual authors, generally sociologists at large urban universities, published a great mass of books on the social ills of the country.

Policemen were often roundly criticized for their handling of riots and demonstrations as well as for "failing to relate" to their communities. Some of the criticism was warranted, but much of it was shrill, unreasonable, and of questionable value. A favorite tactic of a riot commission was to blame equally the police and their adversaries, then warn that the only way to prevent a future occurrence was to appropriate massive sums of money to alleviate social miseries.

It did not take long for Presidential commissions to fall into disrepute with the citizenry who were too upset about crime and violence to look upon the perpetrators as victims. One commission, however, did gain acceptance, not only from the public and the politicians but also from the criminal justice community it had been assigned to investigate.

In the summer of 1965 President Lyndon Johnson established the President's Commission on Law Enforcement and Administration of Justice. The commission was chaired by Nicholas Katzenbach. An impressive array of advisors and consultants were involved in the investigations, and in February of 1967 the commission released its general report, *The Challenge of Crime in a Free Society,* which was soon followed by task force reports on the police, the courts, corrections, juvenile delinquency and youth crime, organized crime, an assessment of crime, science, and technology, narcotics and drugs, and drunkenness.

**Task Force Report: The Police** contained a thoughtful analysis of police problems and offered reasonable solutions to them. The approach was conservative; the language was guarded, and criticism was tempered by reason. The subjects of the report, the nation's police, were criticized but not attacked. Missing was the flamboyancy that had been the stock in trade of other commissions. Some of the commission's most noteworthy findings and recommendations follow.

1. The police were isolated from the communities they had sworn to serve, and from other components in the criminal justice system. Police science and law enforcement programs were adding to this isolation by offering courses so technical and vocational in nature that classes were

    attended primarily by policemen.

2. City officials had all but abdicated their responsibilities for running police agencies by delegating that responsibility to police chiefs.
3. Police chiefs were often appointed because of demonstrated skill as investigators rather than for administrative competence.
4. Police executives had failed to assume their roles as major policymakers.
5. Fresh blood should be infused into police departments by creating new entry level classifications, and by allowing lateral entry. Minority recruitment should be emphasized.
6. Minimum training and educational requirements should be established for all levels of officers.
7. Formal community relations and internal investigating units should be created.
8. Fragmented local police services should be pooled or consolidated in order to eliminate waste and duplication.

The President's Crime Commission was successful primarily because it was a team effort by a staff eminently qualified to engage in the type of activity for which they were chosen. No single individual, group, or social philosophy dominated the commission. While other commissions were often referred to by the name of their chairmen (i.e. Kerner Commission, Walker Report, Eisenhower Commission), the President's Commission on Law Enforcement was consistently referred to by its designated name, not by the name of its chairman or dominant member.

### THE POLICE REACT

Many police administrators throughout history have had the will to reform their departments, but without the assistance of higher governmental authorities and the application of significant amounts of money, plans could not be operationalized. However, in the sixties, especially during the last third of the decade, law enforcement began making real progress toward that long sought goal—professionalization. In the face of tremendous obstacles and under attack from without, the nation's police made astounding progress. From a craft to a profession? Not quite, but at least the goal was attainable; and what was more important, the police, including the rank-and-file, knew it. Led by the International Association of Chiefs of Police, furnished with a blueprint for reform by a Presidential Commission, and financed by a Federal anticrime package, the police moved forward with enthusiasm.

### The Role of the IACP

In 1962 Quinn Tamm, formerly an assistant director with the FBI, was appointed Executive Director of the International Association of Chiefs of Police. That year the Institute for Police

In 1962 Quinn Tamm was appointed Executive Director of the International Association of Chiefs of Police. Under Tamm's leadership, the IACP has been a positive force for meaningful police reform. *(Courtesy of the IACP)*

Management was formed to help raise funds for the Association. The role of the Field Operations Division, which had been created in 1960, was expanded and teams of consultants were sent to conduct management and reorganizational studies for police departments, both large and small, in forty states. The IACP offered a source of professional advice and knowledge, plus an outside perspective of police operations, that were unavailable elsewhere. Hundreds of law enforcement agencies, including those in Baltimore, Boston, Chicago, Cincinnati, Dallas, Pittsburgh, Seattle, and Washington made use of this service, and no community to which IACP consultants were dispatched was quite the same after a survey. The Association founded a major library and research center and a Management and Research Division. Besides providing technical assistance, the IACP was a major source of professional ideas and judgment, and a moral force which helped the police grow and expand during a time of strife.

## The Omnibus Crime Control and Safe Streets Act of 1968

In 1968 the Congress passed the Omnibus Crime Control and Safe Streets Act, the most comprehensive piece of crime legislation in the nation's history. Although some sections of the bill applied to Federal policing, the real significance of the measure was in its recognition that law enforcement was primarily a local function and that fragmented crime efforts had to be better financed and coordinated. The Law Enforcement Assistance Administration (LEAA) was established within the Department of Justice and those police departments which had wanted to professionalize but could not because they lacked the funds, were provided with the resources to do so. Planning grants were disbursed to states to establish state planning agencies whose task was to draw up comprehensive programs aimed at improving law enforcement and criminal justice. Regional planning councils were set up within the states. When the planning agencies were operationalized, they submitted their proposed programs to LEAA, which then funded them through block action grants. Congress also authorized the Law Enforcement Assistance Administration to make discretionary grants (action grants given to cities, states, or agencies which had programs approved). Programs spanned the full spectrum of criminal justice activities. In Florida, for example, both hardware and software programs were undertaken as money was provided for cadet programs, special crime-fighting units, burglary-robbery prevention programs, community-relations activities, halfway houses, an organized crime and racketeering strike force, training programs, and a state uniform-crime-reporting system, to mention but a few federally funded projects.

In what could become the most far-reaching and far-sighted Federal program, the Office of Academic Assistance (OAA) was formed within the Law Enforcement Assistance Administration to administer the Law Enforcement Education Program (LEEP). LEEP provided financial aid to students enrolled in colleges and universities who upon graduation pledged to seek careers in criminal justice. Loans of up to $1,800 per academic year were made available to pre-service students, while grants of up to $300 per semester were made available to in-service students working in criminal justice agencies. In LEAA's first year, 1969, its total budget was $63 million. In 1970 LEAA's budget was $268 million: $184,522,420 of which was spent for block action grants; $31,999,760 for discretionary grants; $29.9 million for planning grants, and $18 million for academic assistance.

## Community Relations Programs

Municipal police departments, especially those serving urban areas, moved to implement meaningful community relations programs, some of which were funded by Federal grants, but most of which were locally sponsored and run. Permanent departmental community-relations units became popular, and their numbers burgeoned during the decade, especially in the post-1966 period. Towns and cities created programs of real and lasting significance. The Philadelphia Police Department began sponsoring "town hall" meetings to which citizens were invited to participate in an open forum. Storefront centers were opened in Oakland, New York, and dozens of other cities. The St. Louis Police Department, a leader in the field, developed more than a dozen community-based programs designed to reach every citizen in the city regardless of race, sex, age, occupation, or social class. Policemen in Dallas embarked on an experimental program to educate elementary school children about the evils of crime. The Monterey Park,

California, Police Department began dispatching beat patrolmen to meet and greet new arrivals to the community.

Police in the 1960s began a national movement to chip away at the iceberg of isolation that had been building up over the decades. The problem was acute and one that could not be solved in short order because of its long-standing existence. But progress was made as police departments showed that they had the will and the enthusiasm to attack an issue of major social importance.

## Nonlethal Weapons

Police officers had come under a good deal of criticism for their use of lethal weapons in the apprehension of felons and in the handling of civil turmoil, even though official inquiry into these actions exonerated the police from blame in the overwhelming majority of cases. Groups of citizens demanded that the police adopt nonlethal weapons in addition to conventional tear gas canisters and projectiles, a cry welcomed by the police who for years had sought, with little success, the development of such weaponry. Private industry, in response to this need, engaged in crash programs aimed at producing nonlethal weapons. The police adopted these devices as fast as they could be perfected and tested for efficiency, effectiveness, and safety.

The first contemporary nonlethal weapon adopted by a significant number of police agencies was a small aerosol spray can containing a potent chemical agent that caused extreme irritation and temporary incapacitation when sprayed in an attacker's face. The device was a major breakthrough in police weaponry because it offered, for the first time, an inexpensive, portable nonlethal weapon which could be carried by individual officers for use in close contact work. The police came under some early criticism for adopting the weapon when it was alleged that eye damage could result if it was misused. However, many departments drafted strict policies limiting usage, while pointing out, rather effectively, the dangers involved in alternate apprehension devices—firearms and nightsticks. In time the vast majority of citizens accepted the device as a necessary and desirable weapon, and the black-sheathed aerosal can fastened to officers' leather gear became a familiar sight to the public.

To combat mob violence, a device called "pepper fog" was

adopted by scores of state and local agencies. The "pepper fog" was a machine that sprayed thousands of cubic feet of tear gas per minute over an area, but which could be held by one man. The weapon was battery-operated and it too became a familiar sight at the apex of police riot squad and crowd-control formations.

Although the development of chemical agents received first priority from private manufacturers and police administrators, other nonlethal weapons began appearing on the scene, albeit on an experimental basis. A tranquilizer gun that was designed to incapacitate people in much the same way that animals were temporarily disabled was tested, but a seemingly endless series of operational problems kept it from being perfected. A weapon called the "stun gun" was developed, which was a special shoulder weapon that fired a flat, circular disc of woven material, filled with bird shot—a "stun bag." The blow delivered by the projectile was heavy but nonlethal. Other devices that made an appearance during the decade included chemical dye which could be sprayed on rioters during the height of action for later identification, a slippery substance called "banana peel" which could be applied to city streets to prevent rioters from achieving personal mobility, and an electronic device which produced a loud sound that disbursed rioters without causing permanent ear damage.

## Advanced Technology

Unlike other eras, the police in the 1960s showed no reluctance to adopt technological innovations and adapt them to fit their peculiar circumstances. Record-keeping functions were updated. Police cars were fitted with special accessories. Crime laboratories were opened and stocked with sophisticated equipment. Fragmented police agencies, some 40,000 strong, moved to lessen their isolation from one another by creating computer-based information systems and advanced communications centers.

At the Federal level, the FBI in 1965 began to develop its National Crime Information Center (NCIC), an operational information systems program. Operationalized in 1967, the NCIC collected information on wanted persons, stolen vehicles and stolen property, and provided police terminals to those communities and states which wanted to participate.

Local and state agencies also created information systems,

A view of the FBI National Crime Information Center located at FBI Headquarters, Washington, D.C. Employe in foreground is operating the control
typewriter, and viewed at the right is the control console for the Center.
*(Courtesy of the FBI)*

Michigan founded the Law Enforcement Information Network
(LEIN). The California Highway Patrol began a statewide file of
stolen vehicles called Autostatis. A regional records system was
conceived in the San Francisco Bay area. This system, the Police
Information Network (PIN), was to become statewide in scope.
Communities pioneering in establishing like systems included New
York, Chicago, St. Louis, and Los Angeles.

Police agencies also built and staffed modern police communications centers whose primary function was to make
maximum use of field units. As the decade ended there seemed to
be a trend toward equipping patrolmen with miniaturized trans-
ceivers so that officers could leave their cars without losing
communications contact.

Police agencies followed the lead of the New York and Los
Angeles Police Departments and helicopters and airplanes were
pressed into service for patrol and investigative work. By the end
of the decade, hundreds of police aircraft had been commissioned
by municipal police departments, sheriffs departments, and state
agencies.

## Police Educational Programs

Prior to the establishment of the Law Enforcement Assistance
Administration, the education of policemen and prospective police
officers was a sometime thing which was systematically undertaken in but one state—California. Scattered communities across

the country were admittedly enthusiastic about higher education for policemen, but these cities and towns were in no way indicative of the norm. At the heart of the problem was economics. Early studies indicated that because of low pay, most line officers were forced to work second jobs. To give up this extra source of income to pursue an expensive and time-consuming educational program was too much to ask of officers, who often worked rotating shifts, making a difficult idea almost impossible. In California this problem was less acute, as police salaries were significantly higher than those in the rest of the nation, the policy of departmental educational incentives was widespread, and junior colleges were tuition-free, with only a minimal charge for education at state colleges and universities. With the advent of LEEP, college education became available for the first time to officers throughout the country, and colleges and universities, in response to a felt need, began opening their doors to policemen as students for the first time.

From 1960 to 1967 the number of college programs for police increased from about 100 to 234. From 1967 to 1969 college police programs increased to 409, containing 32,000 student majors. By 1970 no less than 890 colleges had applied for and received LEEP funds. As a new decade dawned, other states, notably Florida, Georgia, Illinois, New York, Texas, and Washington, challenged California's leadership in law enforcement education.

## Police Training

Law enforcement training improved during the decade, but not enough to keep abreast of the increasing complexity of the police task. Recruit training expanded greatly as eight states followed California's primacy and passed minimum standards legislation. But this expansion was a relative thing as some departments went from ten hours of recruit training to two hundred hours of training, a big statistical jump, though not nearly an acceptable one. As far as in-service training was concerned, a Ford Foundation survey found it "more a wish than a reality."

## Administrative Innovations

Municipal police executives, assisted by the International Association of Chiefs of Police, the President's Commission on Law

Enforcement, and the Law Enforcement Assistance Administration, sought to upgrade the structure and function of their departments through administrative innovations. Principles of sound management were utilized to maximize efficiency. Police agencies found that increased citizen demands made it necessary to form certain specialized units. As a result, community-relations sections, internal-affairs units, staff-inspectional services, planning and research divisions, legal-advisor staffs, task force patrols, intelligence components, and security sections were created by most major departments, with even smaller agencies engaging in specialization, but to a lesser degree.

## CONCLUSION

Policemen in the 1960s were subjected to extreme social pressure and some of the most deliberately provocative actions in history. They responded by effecting meaningful internal reforms. The educational level of officers was uplifted. Training was improved. Advanced technology was employed. Leadership was strengthened. A group of very able and talented police administrators arose to lead their departments toward professionalization, men who seemed destined to join the Savages, the Vollmers, the Wilsons, and the Parkers as police giants—Frank Rizzo, Philadelphia; Curtis Brostron, St. Louis; Charles R. Gain, Oakland; S. R. Schrotel, Cincinnati; E. Wilson Purdy, Dade County, Florida; Clarence Kelley, Kansas City; Thomas Reddin, Los Angeles.

The decade of the 1960s was the most fruitful one in the history of American law enforcement. It has been said that more was done to upgrade the police during these ten years than during the preceding fifty years. Possibly, but there is a good deal of progress yet to be made, especially in the areas of community relations and training. The old problem of trying to professionalize the police without isolating them from the community is yet to be answered satisfactorily. Another question that must be resolved is the issue of police militancy. If it is allowed to continue in its more extreme forms, then the movement toward professionalizaion could be slowed. But men of competence and goodwill are working long and hard on these problems, and the police are forging ahead, honestly trying to do a difficult and dangerous job under trying circumstances, and trying to win public support for their actions.

# BIBLIOGRAPHY

## BOOKS

Germann, A.C., Day, Frank D., and Gallati, Robert, R.J., *Introduction to Law Enforcement and Criminal Justice* (Springfield: Charles C Thomas, Publisher, 1970).

Ferguson, Wallace K., and Bruun, Geoffrey, *A Survey of European Civilization: Ancient Times to 1520,* 4th. ed. (Boston: Houghton Mifflin Co., 1969).

Liversidge, John, *Britain in the Roman Empire* (New York: Frederick Praeger, Publisher, 1968).

Saklatvala, Beram, *The Origins of the English People* (New York: Taplinger Publishing Co., 1969).

Romier, Lucien, *A History of France* (New York: St. Martins Press, 1966).

Grob, Gerald, N., and Beck, Robert N. *American Ideas,* Vol. 1 (New York: The Free Press, 1963).

Hawke, David, *The Colonial Experience* (New York: The Bobbs—Merrill Company, 1966).

Osgood, Herbert, L., *The American Colonies in the Seventeenth Century* (Gloucester: Peter Smith, 1957).

Savage, Edward, H., *Police Records and Recollections* (Boston: John P. Dale & Company, 1873).

Earle, Alice Morse, *Curious Punishments of Bygone Days* (Montclair, N.J.: Patterson Smith Publishing Corp. Originally published in 1896, reprinted in 1969).

Reith, Charles, *A Short History of the British Police* (London: Oxford University Press, 1948).

Richardson, James F., *The New York Police* (New York: Oxford University Press, 1970).

Sullivan, John L., *Introduction to Police Science* (New York: McGraw Hill, Inc., 1966).

Current, Richard T., Williams, T. Harry, and Friedel, Frank, *American History:* a Survey (New York: Alfred A. Knopf, 1964).

Lane, Roger, *Policing the City—Boston: 1822-1855* (Cambridge: Harvard University Press, 1967).

Mott, Frank Luther, *The News in America* (Cambridge: Harvard University Press, 1952).

Reith, Charles, *A New Study of Police History* (London: Oliver and Boyd, 1956).

Lofton, John, *Justice and the Press* (Boston: Beacon Press, 1966).

Smith, Bruce, *The State Police* (New York: The Macmilliam Co., 1925).

Owings, Chloe, *Women Police* (Montclair, N.J.: Patterson Smith Publishing Corp. Originally published in 1925, reprinted in 1969).

Eldefonso, Edward, Coffey, Richard, and Grace, Richard C., *Principles of Law Enforcement* (New York: John Wiley and Sons Inc., 1968).

Leonard, V.A., *Police Organization and Management* (Brooklyn: The Foundation Press, 1951).

Gammage, Allen Z., *Police Training in The United States* (Springfield: Charles C Thomas, Publisher, 1963).

Merz, Charles, *A Dry Decade* (Seattle: University of Washington Press, 1969).

Clark, Norman H., *The Dry Years and After: Prohibition and Social Change in Washington* (Seattle: University of Washington Press, 1965).

Shay, Frank, *Judge Lynch: His First Hundred Years* (Montclair, New Jersey: Patterson Smith Publishing Corp. Originally published in 1938, reprinted in 1969).

Kefauver, Estes, *Crime in America* (New York: Greenwood Press Publishers, 1968).

Vollmer, August, *The Police and Modern Society* (Berkeley: University of California Press, 1936).

Karlen, Delmar, et al:, *Anglo American Criminal Justice* (New York: Oxford University Press, 1968).

Leuchtenburg, William E., *Franklin D. Roosevelt and The New Deal* (New York: Harper and Row, Publishers, Inc., 1963).

Clinard, Marshall B., *The Black Market* (Montclair, N.J.: Patterson Smith Publishing Corp. Originally published in 1952, reprinted in 1969).

Overstreet, Harry, and Overstreet, Bonaro, *The FBI in Our Open Society* (New York: W.W. Norton and Co., Inc., 1969).

Wilson, O.W., *Parker on Police* (Springfield: Charles C Thomas, Publisher, 1957).

Smith, Ralph Lee, *The Tarnished Badge* (New York: Thomas Y. Crowell Co., 1965).

Bopp, William J., *The Police Rebellion* (Springfield: Charles C Thomas, Publisher, 1971).

Flynn, John J., and Wilkie, John E., *History of the Chicago Police* (New York: Arno Press. Originally published in 1887, reprinted in 1971).

Hamilton, Mary E., *The Policewoman: Her Service and Ideals* (New York: Arno Press. Originally published in 1924, reprinted in 1971).

Harrison, Leonard V., *Police Administration in Boston* (Cambridge: Harvard Law School, 1934).

McAdoo, William, *Guarding a Great City* (New York: Arno Press. Originally published in 1906, reprinted in 1971).

Mayo, Katherine, *Justice to All: The Story of the Pennsylvania State Police* (New York: Arno Press. Originally published in 1917, reprinted in 1971).

Woods, Arthur, *Policewoman and Public* (New York: Arno Press. Originally published in 1919, reprinted in 1971).

Fosdick, Raymond B., *American Police Systems* (New York: The Century Co., 1921).

Winsor, Justin, *The Memorial History of Boston,* Vol. 3 (Boston, 1881).

Sprogle, Howard O., *The Philadelphia Police: Past and Present* (Philadelphia, 1887).

International City Managers Association, *Municipal Police Administration,* 5th ed. (Washington: ICMA, 1961).

Walling, George W., *Recollections of a New York Police Chief* (New York: 1887).

Hafen, Leroy R., and Rister, Carl Coke, *Western America,* 2nd ed. (Englewood Cliffs, N.J.: Prentice Hall, Inc. 1950).

Gilmore, N. Ray, and Gilmore, Gladys, *Readings in California History* (New York: Thomas Y. Crowell Co., 1966).

Weston, Paul B., and Wells, Kenneth M., *Criminal Investigation* (Englewood Cliffs, N.J.: Prentice-Hall, Inc. 1970).

Breihan, Carl W., *Jesse James* (New York: Frederick Fell, Inc. 1953).

Bruce, Robert V., *1877: Year of Violence* (New York: Bobbs-Merrill, 1959).

Cherrington, Earnest H., *The Evolution of Prohibition in the United States of America* (Montclair, N.J.: Patterson Smith Publishing Corp. Originally published in 1920, reprinted in 1969).

Whitlock, Brand, *On the Enforcement of Law in Cities* (Montclair, N.J.: Patterson Smith Publishing Corp. Originally published in 1913, reprinted in 1969).

Reckless, Walter C., *Vice in Chicago* (Montclair, N.J.: Patterson Smith Publishing Corp. Originally published in 1933, reprinted in 1969).

Semmes, Raphael, *Crime and Punishment in Early Maryland* (Montclair, N.J.: Patterson Smith Publishing Corp. Originally published in 1938, reprinted in 1970).

Goebel, Julius, Jr., and Naughton, T. Raymond, *Law Enforcement In Colonial New York* (Montclair, N.J.: Patterson Smith Publishing Corp. Originally published in 1944, reprinted in 1970).

Coleman, Walter J., *Labor Disturbances in Pennsylvania 1850-1880* (New York: Arno Press. Originally published in 1936, reprinted in 1969).

Lane, Winthrop D., *Civil War in West Virginia* (New York: Arno Press. Originally published in 1921, reprinted in 1969).

Levinson, Edward *I Break Strikes!* (New York: Arno Press. Originally published in 1935, reprinted in 1969).

Socialist Publishing Society, *The Accused and The Accusers* (New York: Arno Press. Originally published in 1887, reprinted in 1969).

Stein, Leon, and Taft, Phillip, ed. *The Pullman Strike* (New York: Arno Press. Originally published in 1914, reprinted in 1969).

Hichborn, Franklin, *The System* (Montclair, N.J.: Patterson Smith Publishing Corp. Originally Published in 1915, reprinted in 1969).

Foess, Claude M., *Calvin Coolidge* (Boston: Little Brown and Co., 1940).

Graper, Elmer D., *American Police Administration* (New York: The Macmillian Co., 1921).

## GOVERNMENTAL AND QUASI-GOVERMENTAL DOCUMENTS

Presidents Commission on Law Enforcement and Administration of Justice, *Task Force Report: The Police* (Washington: U.S. Government Printing Office, 1967).

National Commission on the causes and prevention of Violence, *Violence in America* (New York: Signet Books, 1969).

U.S. Census Bureau, *General Statistics of Cities* (1915) (Washington: U.S. Census Bureau, 1915).

New York Police Department, *Semi-Annual Report of the Police Commissioner of New York* (New York: New York Police Department, 1918).

National Commission on Law Observance and Enforcement, George Wickersham, Chairman, (1931).
Report No. 1, *Preliminary Report on Prohibition.*
Report No. 2, *Enforcement of the Prohibition Laws of the United States.*
Report No. 11, *Lawlessness in Law Enforcement.*
Report No. 14, *Police.*

Illinois Association for Criminal Justice, *The Illinois Crime Survey* (Montclair, N.J.: Patterson Smith Publishing Corp. Originally published in 1929, reprinted in 1969).

Citizens Police Committee, *Chicago Police Problems* (Montclair, N.J.: Patterson Smith Publishing Corp. Originally published in 1931, reprinted in 1969).

National Popular Government League, *Report Upon the Illegal Practices of the U.S. Department of Justice* (New York: Arno Press. Originally published in 1920, reprinted in 1969).

The Cleveland Foundation, *Criminal Justice in Cleveland* (Montclair, N.J.: Patterson Smith Publishing Corp. Originally published in 1922, reprinted in 1969).

Missouri Association for Criminal Justice, *The Missouri Crime Survey* (St. Louis, Missouri, Association for Criminal Justice, 1926).

Federal Bureau of Investigation, *Uniform Crime Reports 1969* (Washington: U.S. Government Printing Office, 1970).


## DEPARTMENTAL HISTORIES

Cincinnati Police Department
New York Police Department
Flint, Michigan, Police Department
Kansas City Police Department
Detroit Police Department
San Francisco Police Department
Los Angeles Police Department
Chicago Police Department
Philadelphia Police Department

Berkeley Police Department
Baltimore Police Department
St. Louis Police Department
Fitchburg, Massachusetts, Police Department
New Orleans Police Department
San Antonio Police Department
Wichita Police Department
Tucson Police Department
Texas Department of Public Safety
California Highway Patrol
Pennsylvania State Police
New York State Police
International Association of Chiefs of Police
United States Department of Justice
United States Department of the Treasury
Albuquerque Police Department
Maryland State Police
Los Angeles County Sheriff's Department

# NAME INDEX

# SUBJECT INDEX